CREATIVE YOGURT COOKING

Ethel Lang Graham

WEATHERVANE
BOOKS

In appreciation. . .

With many thanks and grateful appreciation to my husband, Dave, and children, Steve and Susan, for their helpfulness and creative suggestions . . . and to many friends, neighbors, and my co-workers at the University of Maryland who contributed their ideas and offered much encouragement during the writing of this book.

Library of Congress catalog card number: 78-57546
ISBN: 0-517-259052
Published under arrangement with Ottenheimer Publishers, Inc.
Printed in the United States of America.

contents

introduction

Yogurt has been in existence for thousands of years. Its use was first recorded in the Old Testament, although it has probably been used as a food since the time man began to consume the milk of other animals.

Unpasteurized, unrefrigerated, fresh warm milk left to stand in a warm climate turns to yogurt. Bacteria present in the warm, unheated milk ferment the sugar (lactose) in milk to lactic acid. When sufficient amounts of lactic acid have formed throughout the milk, the milk protein (casein) coagulates. The entire batch of milk becomes firm and develops a tart taste.

Today many Americans are rediscovering yogurt and developing a liking for its unique flavor, enjoyed for so many centuries by peoples in Asia and the Middle East. Because of the rapidly increasing interest in natural foods, Americans are consuming more and more yogurt and developing ingenious ways to incorporate it into their diets.

commercial yogurt manufacturing

For reasons of safety, modern-day yogurt is made from pasteurized milk. After pasteurization, selected bacteria are added to milk to ferment it to yogurt. Cultures of *Lactobacillus bulgaricus* and *Streptococcus thermophillus* are usually selected because these particular strains of bacteria seem to produce the most pleasing flavor and firmness without contributing an undesirable, excessively sour taste to yogurt.

The innoculated, warm pasteurized milk is poured into containers and capped. If preserves are used, they are first pumped into the bottoms of the cups. If flavorings and sugars are used, these may be added to the milk along with the cultures.

The containers of cultured milk are held at 112°F for several hours. This is the ideal temperature for the bacteria to grow, multiply, and produce the lactic acid that thickens and sours the milk. The yogurt is then chilled to 45°F and marketed. Yogurt will keep well for about a week in the refrigerator after the expiration date stamped on the package. This date usually indicates when yogurt is 1 week old.

Avoid purchasing yogurt that has been pasteurized *after* culturing if you feel yogurt-forming bacteria are beneficial. Heat of pasteurization prolongs the shelf-life but kills the bacteria present.

making yogurt at home

If you are a true yogurt devotee, you should be making your own yogurt. Why pay $1.60 or more for a quart of commercially made yogurt when you can make it for little more than the cost of a quart of milk?

For under $10.00 in most discount stores and slightly over $10.00 in department or kitchen specialty stores, you can purchase a handy and attractive electric yogurt-maker with an accurate thermometer. This appliance can be used to take all the guesswork out of controlling the holding or incubation temperatures. It operates on low wattage and uses less than $.01 of electricity to incubate each quart of yogurt properly. The machine will have paid for itself after about 8 quarts of yogurt have been made.

To prepare yogurt at home, begin with 1 quart of skim or whole milk and heat it to the boiling point. Do not scorch it. Heating will destroy any unwanted bacteria present and also cause a firmer curd to form during incubation.

If a skin should form on the milk during heating, it must be removed before stirring in the yogurt or yogurt cultures, because the skin cannot be successfully stirred into the milk.

Cool the hot milk to 105 to 110°F. Be exact! Use a thermometer. Below 90°F, yogurt cultures won't grow; above 115°F, they are destroyed.

Add a packaged culture mixture or a heaping tablespoon of commercially prepared plain yogurt to the warm milk. Be sure not to use a yogurt that was pasteurized after culturing. Since the culture mixtures are so expensive, I strongly recommend the use of plain yogurt. The yogurt, if not over 2 weeks old, contains large numbers of the correct yogurt-forming bacteria. You can use homemade yogurt as a starter for each succeeding batch for about a month. Then other strains of bacteria that are gradually introduced begin to produce flavor and texture changes and you must purchase fresh plain yogurt or a new culture to begin again.

The innoculated milk must be held (incubated) at about 110°F for 6 to 10 hours, until a firm curd forms. If you do not have an electric yogurt-maker, you must at this point devise some scheme for keeping the milk at this temperature, or the bacteria will not multiply, and no yogurt will be produced.

Here are some suggestions:

Pour the innoculated milk into cup-sized jelly or vegetable jars. Cover the jars tightly and immerse them up to their shoulders in a pan of water at 110°F. Let this container sit for 6 to 10 hours in one of the following ways:

1. On a food-warming tray
2. Outside in a warm place on a hot day
3. On an electric hot pad
4. In a gas oven with a pilot light
5. In a slightly warmed electric oven
6. Covered with a blanket near a radiator
7. Over the pilot light on a gas range top

When the yogurt is firm, chill it at once. It will become somewhat firmer in the refrigerator. It is best to chill it overnight before serving. Use homemade yogurt within 2 weeks for best flavor.

Specific directions for making yogurt from various forms of milk are given in the first chapter following this introduction.

The recipes in this book were standardized with homemade yogurt made in a Salton® electric yogurt-maker. Dannon® yogurt was used to introduce the bacteria into the milk. I prefer the flavor and texture of homogenized-milk yogurt and used this as the basis for the recipes here.

is yogurt a health food?

Elie Metchnicoff, a respected Nobel Prize winner for physiology and medicine in 1908, was responsible in a large way for introducing yogurt to the western nations. He was a Russian scientist working in France when he produced a report entitled *The Prolongation of Life.* The report was without scientific basis but aroused much interest.

He stated in this publication that humans die prematurely from auto-intoxication. He believed that putrefactive bacteria growing in the intestinal tract produce harmful toxins that are absorbed into the bloodstream and gradually poison the body. He came to this astonishing conclusion by observing the diets of Bulgarian peasants who were noted for their great longevity.

The Bulgarians consumed about 3 quarts of yogurt a day. He theorized that since putrefactive bacteria will not live in yogurt, the consumption of large quantities of yogurt will prevent auto-intoxication.

His interesting theory has never been proved correct. However, in the early 1900s it certainly did much to popularize yogurt.

Even today it has been noted that the natives of Soviet Georgia and Middle Eastern countries live long, healthful, useful lives. Many remain youthful after 100 years. Scientists do not know the reason for this great longevity, but these people do consume large quantities of yogurt—2 or 3 quarts daily. Undoubtedly, living habits, genetics, and climate are highly influential.

There are many biological and environmental causes of aging. Auto-intoxication from the absorption of intestinal poisons is not considered by today's scientists to be related to longevity.

Should you choose to believe, as Metchnicoff did, that the bacteria in yogurt promote longevity, remember to consume unheated yogurt. Heating destroys the bacteria present.

nutritive value of yogurt

Yogurt contains all the nutrients and the same number of calories as the milk from which it was made. Read the nutritional labels found on most yogurt cartons. You'll find it rich in protein, calcium, riboflavin, and vitamin B_{12}.

It may be helpful to remember that plain yogurt contains only milk and bacteria. Therefore, a cup of yogurt as a substitute for lunch will not stave off hunger pangs for any longer a period of time than an equal quantity of milk. All dairy products, including yogurt, are low in iron. Habitual use of "plain-yogurt-for-lunch" with no other sources of iron (whole-grain breads, cereals, meats, vegetables) included in the meal may not be advisable for women and children prone to iron-deficiency anemia.

When fruit preserves are added to sweeten and flavor yogurt, its caloric value nearly doubles, yet its nutritive value remains almost unchanged. Nutritive values decrease slightly if the preserves actually replace some of the yogurt in the yogurt container. Commercially, the type of yogurt sweetened with preserves is known as Swiss-style yogurt. Read and compare nutritional labels.

For your information, here are some approximate caloric values of 1-cup portions of various foods:

	calories
plain skim-milk yogurt	145
whole-milk yogurt	160
fruit-flavored yogurt	200
Swiss-style yogurt	250
sour cream	495
mayonnaise	1600
French dressing	1040

For weight-watchers, the use of plain yogurt in place of sour cream, mayonnaise, or French dressing results in a smooth dressing, dessert, or sauce with a substantial reduction in the caloric value of a dish. Try the many recipes for low-calorie dips, dressings, desserts, etc. included among the recipes that follow.

other uses for yogurt

Yogurt may be of nutritional value in the diets of persons who experience lactose intolerance and who cannot consume milk without developing gas and abdominal cramps 2 to 4 hours later. These symptoms most often are seen in Blacks or Orientals, although many Caucasians also experience them after consuming 1 or more glasses of milk.

Persons who lack sufficient amounts of the small intestinal enzyme lactose are unable to digest the lactose in milk. When the undigested lactose passes into the large intestinal tract, it causes water to be absorbed into the tract and produces diarrhea. Bacteria soon grow on the lactose and produce the gas that causes painful bloating. Naturally, the individual tends to avoid drinking milk, one of the richest sources of calcium, protein, and riboflavin in the diet.

Since yogurt contains only half the lactose found in milk (the other half having been fermented by yogurt cultures to lactic acid), only small amounts of lactose are needed for its digestion. Yogurt is easily digested by a lactose-intolerant person and supplies all the same nutrients as the milk from which it was made.

Yogurt is often recommended to those who are undergoing long treatment with sulfa drugs or antibiotics. Such medications eventually destroy most of the bacteria that normally exist in the intestinal tract. Some of these bacteria are known to produce vitamin K and several of the B vitamins there. Yogurt can be used to re-establish viable bacteria in the intestinal tract. Whether vitamins produced by these bacteria in the intestines are actually absorbed into the bloodstream in important quantities is open to question. Nevertheless, should you consume yogurt for this purpose, be sure to eat it unheated, as heating destroys the bacteria present.

use of yogurt in recipes

Yogurt is usually served alone, in beverages, with fruit, or as the basis for salad dressings. In this manner none of its living bacteria are destroyed by heating. Yogurt has nearly the thickness of mayonnaise and sour cream but is higher in nutritive value and far lower in caloric value. Combined with salt, spices, and herbs, yogurt forms the basis for delicious salad dressings and low-calorie dips. With a touch of honey and a bit of lemon juice, yogurt is transformed into a creamy fruit-salad dressing.

Frozen in an ice-cream maker with sugar and flavoring, it makes a scrumptuous low-calorie form of "ice cream." Arranged in a parfait glass with layers of fresh fruit, yogurt makes the perfect dessert for dieting family members and friends. Combined with crushed ice and fruit juice, it forms an appealing thick, cool beverage low in calories.

If yogurt is used in hot soups, sauces, baked products, or main dishes, it contributes an interesting, undefinable, tangy taste and imparts a smooth, creamy texture to the dish. Yogurt must be handled correctly when used with hot foods or it will curdle. The network of coagulated milk protein formed during incubation will shrink, curds will form, and liquid whey will separate out—disaster!

Yogurt, if heated alone in a saucepan, will curdle. Placed atop hot vegetables, yogurt will curdle. Handle it properly, and this will not happen.

If you wish to prepare hot yogurt sauces, the yogurt must be thickened as you would thicken a white sauce. It cannot be spiced and seasoned and heated alone, or it will curdle. Follow this book's recipe directions for thickening with a fat and flour paste or by stirring cornstarch, a flour and water paste, or egg yolks into the cold yogurt prior to heating. These will prevent separation. Do not overheat.

Yogurt may be stirred into hot soups or gravies, provided the soup or gravy has been thickened first with a flour and water paste, cornstarch paste, etc. Be sure not to overheat after its addition.

homemade yogurt

low-calorie plain skim-milk yogurt

When made from 1% skim milk, yogurt contains only about 100 calories per cup. The body is a bit thin and you actually may prefer to use a 2% skim milk for a creamier texture. The caloric value of the yogurt would then be close to 120 calories per cup. Read the nutritional label for the exact calorie content.

Yield: 4 cups

> **1 quart skim milk (1 or 2%)**
> **1 heaping tablespoon unpasteurized yogurt**

Heat milk over moderately high heat until it nearly reaches the boiling point. Remove at once; cool to 110 to 105°F.

Add yogurt; stir or whisk until completely dispersed. Pour into clean jars; incubate at 110 or 105°F for 6 to 10 hours, until firm.

Refrigerate at once. Chill at least 3 or 4 hours before serving or using in a recipe. Yogurt is sweetest when used within several days, but it will keep up to two weeks in the refrigerator.

homemade yogurt

creamy plain skim-milk yogurt

The addition of nonfat dry milk to the skim milk used in preparing yogurt will produce a creamier-textured and perhaps a more acceptable and substantial yogurt. In return for the 20 extra calories in a one-cup serving, the dry milk also increases the protein content of a serving by about 2 grams and contributes additional minerals and vitamins.

Yield: 4 cups

> ⅓ **cup nonfat dry milk solids**
> **1 scant quart skim milk***
> **1 heaping tablespoon plain unpasteurized yogurt**

Dissolve nonfat dry-milk solids in milk; heat, cool, add yogurt, and incubate as directed for Low-Calorie Plain Skim-Milk Yogurt

*Whole milk may be used if calories are not a concern.

thickened plain yogurt

The addition of unflavored gelatin to warmed milk will produce a firmer yogurt after refrigeration. It will also decrease the chances of separation. The gelatin adds only 6 calories per cup. True yogurt afficionados do not enjoy this type of yogurt and prefer the texture of the more natural product.

I recommend this yogurt only for use in frozen yogurt prepared in an ice-cream maker. The added gelatin contributes body and keeps the ice crystals small, for a smooth, velvety texture.

A number of commercial yogurt manufacturers market a gelatin-thickened yogurt. Read the label before buying.

Yield: 4 cups

> **1 envelope unflavored gelatin**
> **1 quart cold whole milk**
> **1 heaping tablespoon plain unpasteurized**
>   **yogurt**

Sprinkle gelatin over about ¼ cup of the cold milk; set aside to soften.

Heat remainder of milk to the boiling point. Add the softened gelatin–milk mixture. Stir well; cool to 110 to 105°F.

Add the yogurt; stir until it has completely dispersed. Pour into clean jars and hold at 110 or 105°F about 6 to 10 hours, until firm.

Refrigerate jars at once for 3 to 4 hours before serving.

rich plain whole-milk yogurt

When made from homogenized milk, 1 cup of plain yogurt contains about 160 calories. Whole-milk yogurt is richer in flavor and thicker than skim-milk yogurt. I prefer this type of yogurt for salad dressings and dips.

Yield: 4 cups

1 quart whole milk
1 heaping tablespoon plain unpasteurized yogurt

Follow the directions for Low-Calorie Plain Skim-Milk Yogurt.

yogurt cottage cheese

Yogurt, when drained of its whey, is very thick and creamy in texture. Seasoned with salt and herbs, it makes a flavorful spread similar to cottage or cream cheese.

Yield: About ⅓ cup for each original cup of yogurt used

1 to 3 cups freshly prepared yogurt
Cheesecloth and colander

Place 2 layers of cheesecloth in a large colander. Gently stir, then pour in the yogurt and allow to drain over a large bowl for about 4 hours. The longer it drains, the thicker it will be. Refrigerate and use within several days. Use as you would cream cheese or cottage cheese.

vanilla yogurt

Yield: 4 cups

1 quart whole milk or 1 quart skim milk plus ⅓ cup nonfat dry milk
1 heaping tablespoon yogurt
⅓ cup sugar
2½ teaspoons vanilla
Dash cinnamon or nutmeg
Shredded coconut (optional)

Heat milk over moderately high heat until it nearly boils. Cool to 115 to 105°F.
Add the yogurt, sugar, and vanilla. Stir until well-blended and sugar is completely dissolved.
Pour into clean jars; hold at 110 to 105° F until firm. Chill 3 to 4 hours before serving.
Garnish yogurt with a dash of cinnamon or nutmeg and a sprinkling of coconut.

coffee yogurt

Yield: 4 cups

1 quart milk	**¼ cup sugar or sugar to taste**
4 heaping teaspoons instant coffee	**1 heaping tablespoon yogurt**

Heat the milk as in the directions for Low–Calorie Plain Skim–Milk Yogurt. Add coffee and sugar. Cool to 110°F. Add yogurt; incubate as directed.

fruit–flavored yogurt

There are numerous good ways to prepare a fruit-flavored yogurt. Addition of fresh fruit in moderate amounts provides the fewest calories and most nutrients. Other choices include addition of fruit preserves, syrups, or extracts and sugar.

fresh or canned fruit

Pureed or chopped fresh or canned fruit may be stirred into chilled prepared yogurt just before serving. Use any amount of fruit you wish; from 2 tablespoons to ½ cup of fruit to each cup of yogurt is usually preferred. If you prepare your own yogurt, the addition of fruit to milk prior to incubation is definitely not advised, for numerous reasons. Pieces of fresh fruit float and darken. The acids in most canned fruits and acids and enzymes in fresh fruits will surely coagulate the milk at once after addition or during the incubation period. Do not use this technique! Add fruit only to prepared yogurt.

jam, jelly, or preserves

If you prepare your own yogurt, place 2 to 3 tablespoons of jam, jelly, or preserves in the bottom of each cup-sized jar before adding the warmed milk and yogurt mixture. Incubate for 6 to 10 hours. The preserves etc. will level out and liquefy somewhat on the jar bottom during incubation. Chill the yogurt; stir up some of the preserves as you eat each spoonful. Do not try to mix preserves, jam, or jelly through the milk prior to incubation. The acids present may curdle the milk during incubation.

fruit-flavored syrups

Add these to prepared yogurt only. Added to the warm-milk mixture, they will curdle the milk during incubation.

fruit-flavored extracts

Add your favorite extract, about ½ teaspoonful per cup of milk, prior to incubation. About 2 tablespoons of sugar or honey may be added as well. This procedure will not curdle milk.

fruit-flavored drink-mixes

Add 1 to 2 tablespoons of a pre-sweetened drink mix such as a lemonade mix, to each cup of chilled, prepared plain yogurt. Stir briefly to mix before eating.

date–nut yogurt

Yield: 2½ cups

> **2 cups plain yogurt**
> **¼ cup chopped dates**
> **¼ cup raisins**
> **3 tablespoons sugar or honey**
> **1 teaspoon vanilla**
> **¼ teaspoon cinnamon**
> **Dash nutmeg**
> **¼ cup chopped walnuts**

Combine all ingredients; chill before serving. Top with coconut, if desired.

honey stir-up yogurt

Yield: 4 or 5 cups

Select either a skim or whole-milk plain yogurt recipe. Place 1 to 2 tablespoons of honey in the bottom of 5 empty cup-sized jars. After cooling the milk and adding the yogurt, slowly pour the yogurt-milk mixture over the honey in each jar. Cover; incubate at 100° F for 6 to 10 hours, as directed. Chill yogurt 3 to 4 hours.

Serve yogurt in the jar. Stir up some of the honey with each spoonful.

alpine breakfast

Yield: Serves 1 person

½ banana, sliced
1 tablespoon lemon juice
½ slice canned pineapple
¼ cup red currants, raspberries, or blueberries
⅓ to ½ cup rolled oats
½ cup plain or fruit-flavored yogurt
2 tablespoons cottage cheese
1 tablespoon rum or a drop of rum flavoring
⅛ teaspoon ground ginger
1 tablespoon honey

Sprinkle banana with lemon juice.
Cut pineapple into small pieces; set aside a few pieces for use as a garnish.
Mix banana, pineapple, and berries with oats; spoon into bowl.
Blend together yogurt, cottage cheese, rum, ginger, and honey. Pour over cereal; garnish with reserved pineapple.

alpine breakfast

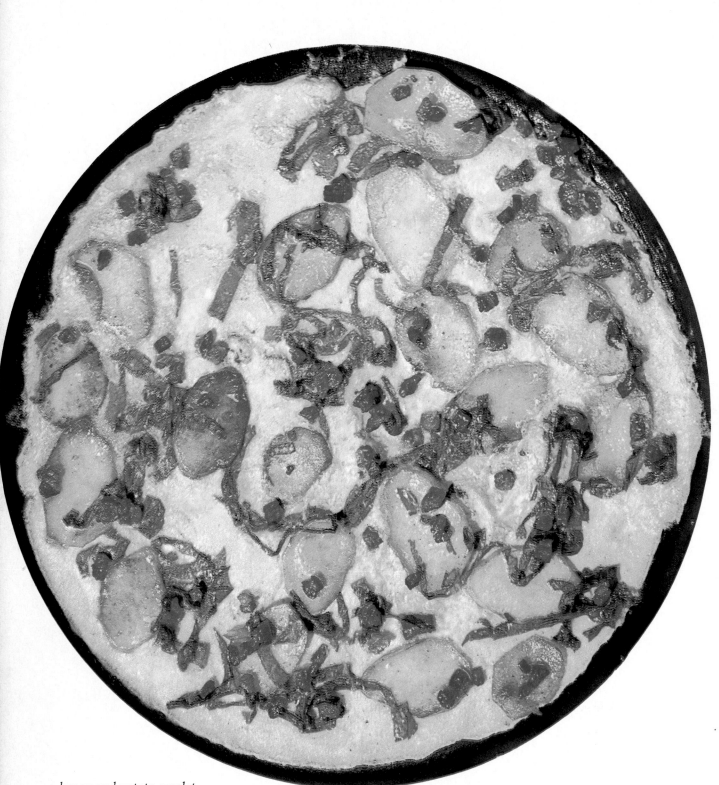

bacon and potato omelet

16

mushroom omelet

Yield: 2 servings

mushroom topping

1 cup sliced fresh mushrooms
2 tablespoons butter or margarine
½ cup plain yogurt
½ teaspoon dillweed

omelet

1 tablespoon butter or margarine
4 eggs
½ teaspoon salt

Prepare topping. Sauté mushrooms in butter in a 10-inch skillet or omelet pan until tender, about 2 or 3 minutes. Remove from pan, cool to room temperature, and add yogurt and dill.

Prepare omelet. Melt butter in the skillet or omelet pan. Lightly mix eggs and salt with a fork; pour into skillet. As edges set, lift gently to allow uncooked portions to run underneath.

When omelet is cooked through but still moist, top with mushroom mixture.

Carefully roll omelet out of pan onto a warm platter.

bacon and potato omelet

Yield: 3 servings

3 slices bacon, cut into small pieces
2 small potatoes, peeled, and sliced
8 fresh spinach leaves, stems removed, and sliced into ¼-inch slices
6 eggs, lightly beaten with a fork
½ cup yogurt
Salt and pepper to taste

In a 10-inch skillet, heat bacon briefly. Add potatoes and fry until bacon is crisp and potatoes are lightly browned; add spinach and remove mixture to a small bowl.

Combine eggs and yogurt, salt and pepper. Pour into skillet. Distribute potato mixture evenly over them. Cook over low heat without stirring. As eggs set on bottom, lift edges and allow uncooked mixture to run underneath. When the omelette is set, fold with a fork and serve immediately.

quickie breakfast-in-a-glass

For a breakfast-on-the run.

Yield: 1 serving

1 cup plain yogurt
1 egg
3 tablespoons wheat germ
3 tablespoons frozen orange-juice concentrate
2 tablespoons honey or light molasses

Combine all ingredients in a blender. Blend until smooth. Serve at once.

ambrosia omelet

Nice for a ladies' luncheon or a summer brunch.

Yield: 2 servings

fruit topping

½ cup yogurt
2 teaspoons sugar
½ cup sliced strawberries
½ cup pineapple tidbits, drained
½ banana, sliced
¼ cup flaked coconut, toasted

omelet

1 tablespoon butter or margarine
4 eggs
¼ teaspoon salt
¼ teaspoon grated lemon peel

Combine ingredients for topping; set aside.
Melt butter in a 10-inch skillet or omelet pan.
Lightly mix eggs, salt, and lemon peel with a fork; pour into skillet. As egg mixture sets, lift the edges to allow any uncooked portions to run underneath.
When omelet is cooked through but still moist, top with fruit mixture. Gently roll omelet out of pan onto a warm platter. Serve at once.

pancakes

Yield: 12 3- to 4-inch pancakes

    2½ cups sifted all-purpose flour*
    4 teaspoons baking powder
    1 teaspoon salt
    ¼ cup sugar
    2 eggs
    3 tablespoons vegetable oil
    1 cup plain yogurt
    1 cup milk

Sift together flour, baking powder, salt, and sugar in a mixing bowl.

Combine eggs, oil, yogurt, and milk. Beat until well-mixed. Pour all at once into dry ingredients.

Stir only until dry ingredients are barely moistened. Batter should be lumpy.

Pour about ¼-cup portions onto a preheated griddle or skillet. Heat until bubbles form on surface. Turn and cook on other side until browned. Serve piping hot.

*2¼ cups whole-wheat flour may be substituted.

appetizers and dips

cottage-cheese tartare

This dish may be served as beef tartar is, as a cocktail appetizer, or as a snack.

Yield: 4 to 6 servings

1 12-ounce container cottage cheese
⅓ cup yogurt
1 tablespoon prepared mustard
Salt and white pepper to taste
2 tablespoons capers
2 or 3 tomatoes, cut into thin wedges
3 or 4 tablespoons chopped chives or thinly sliced scallions
1 large onion, chopped
4 to 6 ounces small cooked shrimp
Paprika
Caraway seeds
Assorted crackers and snack breads

In a blender or food processor cream together cottage cheese, yogurt, and mustard until smooth. Season to taste with salt and pepper.

Arrange capers, tomatoes, chives or scallions, onion, and shrimp on a platter with the tartare. Also have on hand paprika and caraway seeds to be used as a garnish. Serve the tartare on crackers or snack breads. Top with any of the other ingredients, singly or in combination. Sprinkle with paprika or caraway seeds, if desired.

Picture on opposite page: cottage-cheese tartare

seafood cocktail

Yield: 4 servings

1 orange
2 tablespoons kirsch
12 blue grapes, halved,
    seeds discarded
Lettuce leaves
1 small can white asparagus tips
    (optional, but available in
    specialty food stores)
12 ounces canned or cooked
    seafood (shrimp, lobster,
    scallops, or crab meat)

cocktail dressing

¼ cup mayonnaise
¼ cup plain yogurt
1 teaspoon catsup
1 teaspoon prepared horseradish
Freshly ground black pepper
    to taste
Few drops Worcestershire sauce,
    to taste
1 tablespoon lemon juice
Salt and pepper to taste

garnishes

Whole blue grapes
Unpeeled orange slices, halved
Cooked crab claws

Peel orange, removing as much of the white membrane as possible. Cut orange into slices and each slice into quarters. Sprinkle with kirsch.

Prepare dressing by blending together all dressing ingredients.

Arrange orange pieces in 4 champagne glasses lined with lettuce leaves. Add grape halves and asparagus tips. Arrange selected seafood on top. Pour dressing over all.

Serve seafood cocktail at once garnished with whole grapes, half a slice of unpeeled orange, and a crab claw.

22

cottage-cheese appetizers

Yield: Varies

Yogurt Cottage Cheese (see Index)
Chopped herbs to taste
Garlic salt and freshly ground black pepper to taste
Crackers, toast rounds, dark rye bread, etc.

Combine Yogurt Cottage Cheese, your favorite herbs, and seasoned salt. Spread in a thin layer over crackers or snack breads. Cover each with assorted vegetables or toppings, such as:

Cracked black pepper
Shredded carrots
Cress
Sliced cucumber
Sliced hard-cooked eggs
Shredded onion
Chopped parsley
Sliced radishes
Tomato slices

stuffed mushrooms

Yield: 16 to 20

24 medium whole fresh mushrooms
2 cups finely chopped or ground ham
½ cup plain yogurt mixed with 1 tablespoon all-purpose flour
⅓ cup chopped walnuts
1 tablespoon chopped fresh parsley leaves

Remove the stems from the mushrooms.
Combine ham, yogurt, walnuts, and parsley. Place a heaping tablespoon of this mixture in the center of each mushroom cap. Place on a lightly greased baking sheet; bake at 400°F about 12 minutes. Serve hot.

Picture on next pages: yogurt cottage-cheese appetizers

cream-cheese horseradish dip

Yield: About 1¼ cups

> 1 8-ounce package cream cheese
> ½ cup plain yogurt
> 3 tablespoons prepared horseradish
> 1 teaspoon paprika
> Salt and sugar to taste

Blend cream cheese with yogurt and horseradish. Add paprika; season to taste with salt and sugar.

Serve dip with crackers, chips, or vegetable dippers.

apple–nut horseradish dip

Yield: About 1 cup

> 2 apples, peeled and cored
> 1 tablespoon lemon juice
> ¼ cup yogurt
> 1 tablespoon prepared horseradish
> 2 tablespoons minced or ground walnuts

Grate apples; immediately combine with lemon juice to prevent discoloration. Blend in remaining ingredients.

Serve dip at once with chips, crackers, or vegetable dippers.

ham horseradish dip

Yield: About ⅔ cup

> 4 ounces cooked ham
> 1 dill pickle
> ½ cup plain yogurt (may be part mayonnaise)
> 1 tablespoon prepared horseradish
> Drop Tabasco sauce
> Salt and pepper to taste

Finely dice ham and pickle. Combine with yogurt, horseradish, and Tabasco sauce. Season to taste with salt and pepper.

Serve dip at once with crackers, chips, or vegetable dippers.

Pictured from top to bottom:
cream-cheese horseradish dip
apple–nut horseradish dip
ham horseradish dip

blue-cheese and bacon dip

Delicious as a topping on baked potatoes. Bacon may be omitted.

Yield: 1⅓ cups

1 cup plain yogurt
3 ounces blue cheese, crumbled
½ stalk celery, minced
Salt to taste
4 slices bacon, cooked until crisp, crumbled

Combine all ingredients.
Serve dip very cold with chips or vegetable dippers.

famous onion-soup-mix dip

The usual version is made with sour cream that contains over twice as many calories as yogurt.

Yield: 2 cups

1 envelope your favorite brand onion-soup mix
2 cups plain yogurt

Stir together onion-soup mix and yogurt. Chill before serving.
Good with chips, crackers, or vegetable dippers.

guacamole and tortilla-chip dip

Always a favorite at cocktail parties!

Yield: About 1cup

1 large ripe avocado, peeled and pitted
2 to 3 tablespoons plain yogurt
2 teaspoons minced onion
1 medium tomato, chopped
½ teaspoon garlic salt
1 teaspoon lemon juice
Dash lemon pepper (optional)
Tortilla or corn chips

Coarsely mash avocado with a fork. Stir in yogurt and onion. Add tomato, garlic salt, lemon juice, and lemon pepper.
Serve dip at once with chips. Surface of dip may darken if dip is allowed to stand before serving. If this occurs, restir before serving.

zesty apple dip

Yield: About 3 cups

    1 medium onion
    1 large apple, peeled and cored
    2 cups yogurt
    2 tablespoons lemon juice
    2 tablespoons chopped parsley
    Dash Worcestershire sauce
    1 tablespoon catsup
    Drop Tabasco sauce
    Salt to taste

Coarsely grate onion and apple; stir into yogurt. Add remaining ingredients; mix well.

Serve dip with crisp rye crackers or toast points.

susan's mustard dip

Nice with seafoods, zesty crackers, or beef fondue.

Yield: About 1¼ cup

    ½ cup yogurt
    ½ cup mayonnaise
    ¼ cup chopped fresh parsley leaves
    2½ tablespoons prepared mustard
    1 tablespoon lemon juice

Combine all ingredients and chill well before serving.

margaret's chinese-style dip

Dairy foods are not widely used in the Orient, so this dip is not authentically Chinese. It has an Oriental flavor, however.

Yield: 1¼ cups

    1 cup yogurt
    2 tablespoons soy sauce
    2 scallions, very thinly sliced

Combine all ingredients.
Serve dip with Japanese crackers.

seafarers' dip

Great way to use leftover cooked fish.

Yield: About 2 cups

1 3-ounce package cream cheese
1 cup plain yogurt
8 ounces chilled cooked fish, broken into small flakes
2 hard-cooked eggs, chopped
1 scallion, thinly sliced
1 to 2 teaspoons horseradish
½ teaspoon salt

Blend together with a fork the cream cheese and yogurt. Add remaining ingredients; mix until blended.
Serve dip with chips, crackers, or vegetable dippers.

clam dip

Yield: About 1½ cups

1 3-ounce package cream cheese
½ cup yogurt
1 8-ounce can minced clams, drained
1 tablespoon minced scallions or onion
1 teaspoon Worcestershire sauce
Garlic salt to taste
Freshly ground black pepper

Soften the cream cheese with a little yogurt. Add remaining yogurt and other ingredients. Chill well.
Serve dip with chips or vegetable dippers.

curried shrimp dip

For a milder dip, omit the curry powder.

Yield: 1½ cups

1 cup yogurt
1 3-ounce package cream cheese
2 tablespoons minced scallion
1 teaspoon horseradish
1 tablespoon minced fresh parsley leaves
¼ teaspoon Worcestershire sauce
¼ teaspoon celery salt
¼ teaspoon curry powder
8 ounces cooked shrimp, minced
Salt to taste

Gradually stir yogurt into cream cheese with a fork. Add remaining ingredients; chill.
Serve dip with crackers, chips, or vegetable dippers.

dip aux fines herbes

The flavor of this popular dip is similar to that of a popular brand-name spread.

Yield: 1¼ cups

¼ cup butter, softened
2 cloves garlic, crushed or minced
½ cup cottage cheese, drained
½ cup plain yogurt
¼ cup chopped fresh parsley leaves
1 teaspoon salt
Cracked black peppercorns

Combine butter and garlic. Whisk together until well-blended. Add cottage cheese; whisk until smooth. Stir in yogurt, parsley leaves, and salt. Garnish with a sprinkling of cracked peppercorns before serving.
Serve dip with chips, crackers, or vegetable dippers.

creative low-calorie vegetable dip

Dip contains approximately 50 calories per ⅓ cup. Be sure to serve it with cold fresh vegetable dippers, not high-calorie crackers, or you will not have a low-calorie appetizer.

Yield: About 1½ cups

½ cup yogurt
½ cup drained cottage cheese
Choice of one or more of the following vegetables:
    1 stalk celery, minced
    ½ cucumber, coarsely grated
    4 sprigs parsley, finely chopped
    ½ green pepper, minced
    4 to 6 radishes, coarsely grated
    ½ scallion, minced
    3 or 4 fresh spinach leaves, minced
Choice of one or more of the following seasonings:
    1 tablespoon lemon juice or vinegar
    1 teaspoon Worcestershire sauce
    Garlic, onion, or celery salt to taste

Combine the selected ingredients and keep them refrigerated. Serve with crisp, cold vegetable dippers such as:
Whole green beans, tips and stems removed
Carrot and celery sticks
Cauliflower florets
Radish roses
Turnip sticks

avocado soup

Yield: About 4 cups

> 2 ripe, soft avocados, pitted and peeled
> 1 teaspoon lemon juice
> 1 cup cold chicken broth
> 1 cup light cream
> ½ cup plain yogurt
> ½ cup dry white wine
> Salt to taste

Set aside a few thin slices of avocado brushed with lemon juice to use as a garnish. Place remaining avocado in a food processor or blender; blend until smooth.
Add remaining ingredients; blend until smooth.
Serve soup very cold, garnished with reserved avocado slices.

russian borscht

Yield: 4 cups

> 1 No. 2½ can beets, drained, liquid reserved
> 1 clove garlic
> 1 can condensed cream of chicken soup
> 1 can condensed beef consommé
> ½ teaspoon tarragon
> ½ teaspoon chervil
> ½ teaspoon dried parsley leaves
> Salt to taste
> Plain yogurt

Puree beets and garlic clove in an electric blender until very smooth. Add chicken soup; puree until blended.
Combine pureed mixture, beef consommé, herbs, and salt. Chill well in a covered container.
Serve borscht cold in large bowls. Garnish with a dollop of yogurt seasoned to taste with salt.

Picture on opposite page: avocado soup

cream of vegetable soup

Yield: 4 servings

> 1 10-ounce package frozen vegetables (carrots, cauliflower, artichoke hearts,
>   etc.), cooked according to package directions and drained
> 1 10¾-ounce can condensed cream of celery soup
> 1½ cups plain yogurt
> 4 ounces grated cheddar cheese
> Chopped fresh parsley leaves

Combine half of the cooked vegetables with soup, yogurt, and cheese. Blend in a blender until smooth. Pour into saucepan; bring to a boil. Add reserved vegetables. Heat briefly.

Serve soup at once garnished with parsley.

irish chicken soup

A rich chicken soup with a delicate yogurt flavor.

Yield: 6 servings

> 5 cups water
> 1½ teaspoons salt
> 2 pounds chicken parts (wings, necks, backs)
> 2 stalks celery, sliced
> 1 leek, sliced
> 1 large carrot, cubed
> 2 medium potatoes, cubed
> ½ cup peas
> 2 egg yolks
> ¾ cup plain yogurt
> ½ head Bibb lettuce, coarsely chopped

Bring water, salt, and chicken parts to a boil in a large saucepan. Cover; simmer for 1 hour.

Add celery, leek, carrot, and potatoes. Simmer another 20 minutes. Remove chicken; cube meat; return to soup. Add peas; simmer about 8 minutes. Remove scum from surface of soup.

Lightly beat egg yolks; stir into yogurt.

Remove soup from heat; stir in yogurt mixture.

Garnish soup with sliced lettuce. Adjust seasoning. Serve at once.

Picture on opposite page: irish chicken soup

green-onion and cucumber soup

Similar to Iced Cucumber Soup—less garlic flavor.

Yield: 4 or 5 servings

3 eggs
2 cups milk
1 cup plain yogurt
1 cup cold chicken broth
½ cup dry white wine (Chablis is quite good)
2 cups grated, peeled cucumber
3 tablespoons grated green onions (scallions)
1 teaspoon salt
Dash dillweed
Dash paprika

In the top of a double boiler whisk eggs into milk. Heat over hot, not boiling, water until mixture is thickened. (Do not overheat, beyond 185°F, or mixture curdles.) Cool.

Add the yogurt, broth, wine, cucumber, green onions, and salt. Chill well.

Just before serving, garnish each portion with dillweed and paprika.

vichyssoise

Yield: 6 servings

¾ pound leeks, halved lengthwise and sliced thinly
1 medium onion, chopped
2 tablespoons butter
2 large potatoes, peeled and diced
3 cups chicken stock
Salt to taste
2 cups light cream
Dash Tabasco sauce
1 cup plain yogurt
Chopped chives

Heat leeks and onion in butter in a large skillet until transparant; do not brown. Add potatoes, chicken broth, and salt. Simmer until potatoes are tender, about 30 minutes.

Pour soup into blender; puree. Stir in cream and Tabasco sauce. Strain soup through a sieve; chill.

Just before serving, stir in yogurt. Readjust seasoning.

Serve soup very cold, garnished with chopped chives.

Picture on opposite page: vichyssoise

iced cucumber soup

Yield: 6 to 8 servings

>   **2 cups milk**
>   **4 cups plain yogurt**
>   **½ cup dry white wine**
>   **1 tablespoon lemon juice**
>   **1 onion, grated**
>   **1 clove garlic, minced or crushed**
>   **2 large (about 1 pound) cucumbers, unpeeled and finely grated**
>   **Salt and pepper to taste**
>   **Sprigs watercress or parsley (garnish)**

Whisk together the milk and yogurt in a large bowl. Gradually add the wine and lemon juice. Stir in the onion, garlic, cucumbers, salt, and pepper.

Cover; refrigerate for 1 hour before serving.

Garnish soup with cucumber slices and watercress to serve.

iced cucumber soup

fresh mushroom soup

Yield: 4 or 5 servings

¾ pound fresh mushrooms
1 small onion, finely chopped
3 tablespoons butter
4 cups beef stock
3 tablespoons all-purpose flour mixed
    to a paste with ¼ cup cold water

Salt and pepper to taste
2 egg yolks
½ cup plain yogurt
1 teaspoon lemon juice
Chopped fresh parsley leaves
    (garnish)

Set aside a few small whole mushrooms to use as a garnish. Thinly slice the remaining mushrooms.

Heat butter in a large skillet. Brown whole mushrooms, sliced mushrooms, and onion for about 5 minutes. Set aside whole mushrooms.

Add beef broth to mushroom and onion mixture. Add flour–water paste; bring to a boil, stirring occasionally, over moderate heat. Season to taste with salt and pepper. Remove from heat.

Blend yolks into yogurt; stir into soup. (If reheating is necessary, be sure not to boil.) Stir in lemon juice.

Ladle soup into bowls and garnish with whole mushrooms and parsley.

mushroom soup with shrimp

Yield: 4 or 5 servings

¾ pound fresh mushrooms, sliced
3 tablespoons butter
4 cups beef stock
3 tablespoons all-purpose flour mixed
    to a paste with ¼ cup cold water
Salt and pepper to taste
6 to 8 ounces cooked shrimp
2 tablespoons dry sherry

1 teaspoon chopped fresh dill or ½
    teaspoon dried dillweed
2 tablespoons chopped fresh
    parsley leaves
1 egg yolk
½ cup plain yogurt
Parsley for garnish

Brown mushrooms in butter in a large skillet, about 5 minutes. Stir in broth and flour–water paste. Bring to a boil over moderate heat, stirring occasionally. Season to taste with salt and pepper. Add shrimp, sherry, and dill. Heat only until shrimp are warm.

Whisk together egg yolk and yogurt; add to soup.

Serve soup at once garnished with parsley.

Picture on next page: fresh mushroom soup, mushroom soup with ham, mushroom soup with shrimp

mushroom soup with ham

Yield: 4 to 6 servings

> 2 10-ounce cans condensed cream of mushroom soup
> 2 soup cans milk
> 4 slices boiled ham (4 ounces), cut into narrow strips
> 2 egg yolks
> ½ cup plain yogurt
> ¼ cup grated Swiss cheese
> 4 to 6 sprigs fresh parsley

Combine soup, milk, and ham in a large saucepan. Bring to a simmering temperature, stirring occasionally.

Whisk together the yolks and yogurt. Stir into soup. Reheat, if necessary, but do not boil.

Ladle soup into bowls. Sprinkle with cheese and garnish with parsley sprigs.

cream of mushroom soup

Just a touch of yogurt gives this cream soup an unidentifiable, special tangy flavor.

Yield: 4 servings

> 8 to 12 ounces fresh mushrooms, sliced
> 1 small onion, thinly sliced
> ¼ cup butter
> 3½ cups milk
> ⅓ cup all-purpose flour mixed to a smooth
>   paste with ¼ cup cold milk
> 4 chicken bouillon cubes
> Pinch thyme
> Salt and pepper to taste
> ½ cup plain yogurt

Brown mushrooms and onion in hot butter in a large skillet, about 5 minutes. Add milk, flour-milk paste, bouillon cubes, and thyme. Heat over moderate heat, stirring frequently, until soup is thickened and begins to boil. Remove from heat and season to taste with salt and pepper.

Stir a little of the hot soup into the yogurt. Stir this mixture back into the soup.

Serve soup at once. It may be garnished with a sprig of fresh dill.

from bottom, clockwise:
cream of mushroom soup,
cream of mushroom soup with peas,
cream of mushroom soup with tomatoes and ham,
cream of mushroom soup with chicken and red pepper

42

cream of mushroom soup variations

Yield: 4 servings

with peas

> ½ cup frozen, defrosted peas
> 1 recipe Cream of Mushroom Soup
> Curry powder to taste

Add peas to the soup at the time milk is added. Just before serving, sprinkle soup with curry powder.

with tomatoes and ham

> 4 ounces cooked ham, cubed
> 2 tomatoes, peeled, seeds removed, and cubed
> 1 recipe Cream of Mushroom Soup
> Chopped fresh chives

Add ham and tomatoes to hot soup just before serving. Garnish with chives.

with chicken and red pepper

> 4 ounces cooked chicken, slivered
> 1 red (ripe green) pepper or pimiento, slivered
> 1 recipe Cream of Mushroom Soup
> Chopped fresh parsley leaves

Add chicken and pepper to soup at the time milk is added. Before serving, garnish with parsley.

spring salad

Yield: 4 servings

2 kohlrabi, coarsely grated or finely diced
½ pound carrots, coarsely grated or cut into fine strips
1 unpeeled cucumber, thinly sliced
12 radishes, thinly sliced
Watercress (small bunch, if available), chopped

salad dressing

1 cup plain yogurt
1 tablespoon lemon juice
1 to 2 tablespoons honey

garnish

Lettuce leaves
1 hard-cooked egg, cut into wedges

Combine kohlrabi, carrots, cucumber, radishes, and watercress.
Blend together dressing ingredients; pour over vegetables.
Place salad on a bed of lettuce and garnish with wedges of egg.

spring salad

bean-sprout salad

Yield: 6 servings

   1 quart fresh chilled mung-bean sprouts (you may sprout your own from mung-
      bean seeds available in most natural-food stores and some supermarkets)
   2 scallions, very thinly sliced
   1 cup plain yogurt
   1 tablespoon soy sauce
   1 tablespoon dry sherry
   ¼ teaspoon ginger
   Garlic salt to taste

Combine all ingredients. Serve at once.

chef's salad with herb dressing

Yield: 4 servings

   1 small head Bibb lettuce
   2 tomatoes, cut into wedges
   ½ cucumber, sliced
   ¼ cup coarsely grated white or red radishes
   ½ green pepper, cut into strips
   2 ounces cooked chicken or turkey breast, cut into small thin slices
   2 ounces cooked ham, cubed
   2 ounces cheese, cut into thin strips
   2 ounces sardines, drained (optional)
   6 olives, sliced

herb salad dressing

   ½ cup plain yogurt
   1 tablespoon lemon juice
   1 teaspoon chopped parsley
   1 teaspoon dillweed
   Garlic salt to taste

Line individual salad bowls with lettuce leaves torn into bite-size pieces. Arrange tomatoes, cucumber, radishes, and green pepper on top.
   Combine dressing ingredients and pour over arranged salads.
   Add chicken, ham, cheese, and sardines.
   Garnish salad with sliced olives. Serve.

chef's salad with herb dressing

lois' chicken and cashew salad

Cashews and chicken complement each other perfectly.

Yield: 4 servings

2 cups diced, cold cooked chicken meat
½ cup canned small peas, drained
4 ounces fresh mushrooms,
    sautéed in butter
½ cup cashew nuts

¼ cup mayonnaise
½ cup plain yogurt
2 tablespoons dry white wine
Salt and pepper to taste

Combine all ingredients.
Serve salad on a bed of crisp lettuce leaves.

mary's middle-eastern spinach salad

My family definitely prefers this without the mint.

Yield: 6 servings

  1 10-ounce bag fresh spinach, tough stems removed
  2 scallions, thinly sliced
  1 cup plain yogurt
  2 tablespoons olive oil
  2 teaspoons lemon juice
  2 teaspoons minced mint leaves (optional)
  1½ teaspoons salt
  ½ teaspoon freshly ground black pepper
  ¼ cup sliced almonds

Wash spinach well under cold, running water.
Combine scallions, yogurt, olive oil, lemon juice, mint leaves (if used), salt, and pepper.
Drain spinach well. Pour yogurt mixture over spinach; toss to mix.
Sprinkle salad with almonds. Serve at once.

spinach raita salad

Popping mustard seeds sounds like popping corn. The dressing is a bit unusual and very good.

  1 tablespoon vegetable oil
  2 teaspoons mustard seeds
  ½ teaspoon salt
  1 cup plain yogurt
  1 10-ounce bag fresh spinach,
        stems removed, washed and drained

Shake mustard seeds in hot oil in a covered pan over moderate heat until they pop (1 to 2 minutes). Cool.
Combine oil and popped mustard seeds, salt, and yogurt. Add to well-drained spinach. Toss and serve at once.

tomato raita

Raita is an Indian dish of yogurt and vegetables. Serve this version in mid-summer and use vine-ripened tomatoes.

Yield: 4 servings

3 large chilled tomatoes, cubed
1 medium onion, coarsely grated
1 tablespoon minced fresh basil or coriander leaves
1 roasted green chili, chopped (available canned in the Mexican food section of your local supermarket)
¾ cup (or more) plain yogurt
½ teaspoon salt

Combine all ingredients. Serve at once.

succotash raita

Yield: 4 servings

1 cup cooked and chilled lima beans
1 cup cooked and chilled corn
1 cup plain yogurt
½ teaspoon salt
¼ teaspoon curry powder
Chili powder

Combine all ingredients except the chili powder.
Garnish each serving with chili powder when served.

celebrity rice salad

Yield: 6 servings
3 to 4 cups cold, cooked long-grain white rice
½ cup coarsely grated green pepper
2 scallions, very thinly sliced
¼ cup coarsely grated radishes
¼ cup coarsely grated celery
½ cup sweet pickle relish
½ teaspoon (or more) nutmeg
1 teaspoon (or more) curry powder
Dash cloves
½ cup plain yogurt
Salt to taste

Combine all ingredients in a large bowl. Serve at once on a bed of lettuce leaves.

rice salad

Yield: 4 servings

    2 bananas, sliced
    2 tablespoons lemon juice
    8 ounces long-grain rice, cooked according to package directions and chilled
    4 small tomatoes, cut into wedges
    ½ cup canned mandarin-orange sections, drained
    ½ cup cold cooked or canned corn
    4 ounces cold cooked shrimp
    ½ teaspoon dried mint leaves

salad dressing

    ¾ cup plain yogurt
    2 tablespoons mayonnaise
    1 tablespoon orange juice
    1 tablespoon sugar
    ¼ teaspoon salt

Sprinkle banana slices with lemon juice.

Place rice in a serving bowl. Arrange rows of tomatoes, bananas, mandarin orange sections, corn, and shrimp in a starlike pattern on top. Sprinkle with dried mint.

Combine dressing ingredients; pour over rice.

rice salad

spicy garden rice salad

Yield: 4 servings

2 cups cold, cooked rice
1 green pepper diced
3 medium radishes, minced
1 scallion, minced
1 stalk celery, finely chopped
¼ cup pickle relish
1 clove garlic, minced
½ teaspoon nutmeg
1 teaspoon (or less) curry powder
⅛ teaspoon cloves
¼ teaspoon cinnamon
⅓ cup (or more) plain yogurt
Salt to taste

Combine all ingredients. Serve the salad very cold.

wild-rice health salad

Yield: 6 servings

2 cups cold cooked wild rice (4 ounces uncooked)
¼ cup chopped walnuts
½ cup wheat germ
1 cup mung-bean sprouts
½ green pepper, diced
1 scallion, thinly sliced
1 tomato, diced
2 hard-cooked eggs, chopped
1 cup plain yogurt
½ teaspoon dry mustard
1 teaspoon salt

Toss together the wild rice, walnuts, wheat germ, bean sprouts, vegetables, and eggs.

Combine yogurt, mustard, and salt. Pour yogurt mixture over rice. Toss lightly to mix.

Serve salad at once on a bed of lettuce. Sautéed mushrooms may be added to this salad, if you wish.

piquant deviled eggs

Yield: 8 egg halves, filled

4 hard-cooked eggs, halved lengthwise
2 tablespoons plain yogurt
2 tablespoons catsup
2 teaspoons lemon juice
¼ small onion, minced

½ teaspoon mustard
½ teaspoon paprika
Dash Tabasco sauce
Salt and pepper to taste
Chopped chives

Remove yolks from eggs; combine yolks with remaining ingredients, except chives. Mix until well-blended.

Place a heaping spoonful of the mixture into each egg white. Serve eggs, garnished with chopped chives, on a bed of lettuce.

dutch egg salad

Yield: 4 servings

4 hard-cooked eggs, sliced
2 anchovy fillets, diced
1 dill pickle, diced

salad dressing

½ cup plain yogurt
1½ teaspoons prepared mustard
Salt and pepper to taste
Pinch sugar
1 teaspoon lemon juice

garnish

1 hard-cooked egg, sliced
1 medium tomato, sliced
1 anchovy fillet, sliced
2 tablespoons capers
1 small dill pickle, diced
1 pimiento, cut into strips (or ⅓ green pepper)

Combine salad ingredients; place in a small serving bowl.

Combine dressing ingredients; pour over salad.

Arrange egg slices, tomato slices, anchovy, capers, and pimiento on the top of the salad as a garnish. Top tomato slices with chopped pickle. Serve at once.

Picture on opposite page: dutch egg salad

leek and lox salad

Yield: 4 servings

2 leeks
2 or 3 tomatoes
2 hard-cooked eggs
2 to 4 ounces smoked lox
¾ cup plain yogurt
2 tablespoons chopped parsley leaves
1 tablespoon olive oil
1 tablespoon lemon juice
¼ teaspoon dried mustard
1 teaspoon sugar
Salt and pepper to taste

Clean leeks thoroughly; cut into very thin slices. Separate slices into rings.
Peel and cube tomatoes.
Chop eggs coarsely.
Cube lox. Combine all these ingredients.
Stir together yogurt, parsley, oil, lemon juice, mustard, and sugar. Season to taste with salt and pepper. Pour over salad ingredients. Serve at once.

leek and lox salad

turkish cucumber salad

turkish cucumber salad

Yield: 4 servings

> 2 large cucumbers, diced
> 6 ounces baked ham, diced

salad dressing

> 1 cup plain yogurt
> 1 teaspoon prepared mustard
> Dash nutmeg
> Pinch sugar
> Salt and freshly ground black pepper to taste
> Small bunch watercress (if available—easily grown from seed), chopped
> 1 or 2 fresh mint leaves, minced
> 2 tablespoons chopped chives or scallions

garnish

> Watercress
> Parsley leaves

Combine ham and cucumbers.
Prepare dressing by stirring together all ingredients.
Fold ham and cucumbers into dressing.
Serve salad at once garnished with watercress and parsley leaves. Dressing may alternately be used as a topping.

pink stuffed cucumber

pink stuffed cucumber

If you grow long, German cucumbers in your garden, this salad is unusually attractive on a buffet table.

Yield: 4 servings

> 1 long cucumber or 2 6- to 8-inch cucumbers
> 1 tablespoon lemon juice
> ½ teaspoon sugar
> Dash salt
> 3 apples, peeled, cored, and cut into ½-inch cubes
> 2 oranges, skins cut off, pulp cut into ½-inch cubes
> ½ cup plain yogurt
> ¼ cup mayonnaise
> 2 tablespoons catsup
> Orange slices (garnish)

Cut cucumber in half lengthwise. Remove and reserve pulp, leaving a ½-inch-thick shell. Brush shell with lemon juice; sprinkle with sugar and salt. Set aside.

Cut reserved cucumber pulp into ½-inch cubes. Combine with cubed apples and oranges.

Combine yogurt, mayonnaise, and catsup. Pour over cucumber and fruit mixture. Toss gently; spoon into prepared cucumber shell.

Garnish cucumber with orange slices, and serve.

yankee potato salad

Some mayonnaise is necessary for a creamy dressing. Using yogurt only may not be to your liking. Experiment.

Yield: 6 servings

> 4 medium potatoes, boiled, peeled, and cubed
> 1 large stalk celery, diced
> 1 tablespoon fresh parsley leaves, chopped
> ¼ cup mayonnaise
> ¼ cup plain yogurt
> 1 teaspoon salt

Combine all ingredients. Chill before serving.

indian potato salad

Spicy and flavorful.

Yield: 4 servings

> 3 or 4 medium new potatoes, boiled, chilled, and cubed
> ¾ cup plain yogurt
> ⅛ teaspoon curry powder
> ¼ teaspoon chili powder
> 1 roasted green chili, chopped (available canned in Mexican food section of your supermarket)
> 4 large fresh mint leaves, minced
> ½ teaspoon salt

Combine all ingredients; serve at once. Seasonings may be increased for a stronger curry–chili flavor.

summer-garden onion salad

Yield: 6 servings

> 3 cucumbers, peeled and cubed
> 1 Bermuda onion, thinly sliced
> 3 very large tomatoes, peeled and diced
> 1½ teaspoons salt
> 1 cup plain yogurt
> 2 tablespoons lime juice
> 1 teaspoon prepared mustard
> ¼ teaspoon curry powder

Sprinkle prepared vegetables with salt; allow to stand for 30 minutes. Drain away accumulated water.

Combine yogurt, lime juice, mustard, and curry. Pour over vegetables. Toss lightly; serve at once.

grandpa lang's favorite cucumber and radish salad

Try this low-calorie salad when cucumbers are abundant. A cool and refreshing accompaniment to summer meals.

Yield: 4 servings

> 1 large cucumber, peeled if commercially waxed
> Salt
> ½ cup sliced radishes
> ½ cup plain yogurt

Quarter cucumber lengthwise; cut into slices. Salt lightly; allow to stand 20 to 30 minutes. Pour off accumulated water. Add radishes and yogurt. Toss lightly until combined. Salt to taste.

cole slaw

Yield: 4 to 6 servings

> 2 cups shredded cabbage
> ½ cup coarsely grated cucumber
> ¼ cup coarsely grated green pepper
> ¾ teaspoon salt
>
> ¼ teaspoon freshly ground
>   black pepper
> 1 cup (or more) plain yogurt

Combine all ingredients. Serve at once.

radish salad

Yield: 4 servings

> 2 large white radishes
> ½ teaspoon salt
> 1 cucumber, unpeeled
> 1 red cooking apple
> ¾ cup plain yogurt
>
> ½ teaspoon salt
> Freshly ground black pepper
> Dried dillweed or chopped
>   fresh dillweed

Peel and very thinly slice the radishes. Sprinkle with salt; set aside for 15 to 30 minutes.

Very thinly slice the cucumber.

Cut the apple into quarters; remove the core. Cut the quarters into very thin slices.

Drain the accumulated water from the radish slices. Rinse with cold water.

Combine radishes, cucumber, and apple in a serving bowl.

Combine yogurt and salt; pour over vegetables. Sprinkle with pepper and dill.

Picture on opposite page: radish salad

lettuce and fruit salad with sherry dressing

lettuce and fruit salad with sherry dressing

Yield: 4 servings

1 small head iceberg lettuce
½ cup canned mandarin oranges, drained
2 bananas, sliced

sherry salad dressing

½ cup plain yogurt   **1 tablespoon sugar (or sugar to taste)**
1 tablespoon lemon juice   **Dash ginger**
1 tablespoon sherry   **Salt to taste**

Cut lettuce into thin strips. Combine with oranges and bananas.
    Prepare dressing by blending yogurt, lemon juice, and sherry. Season to taste with sugar, ginger, and salt.
    Pour dressing over fruit; serve at once.

fruit and walnut salad

Yield: 4 servings

½ honeydew melon
2 oranges
¼ pound blue grapes
1 small head Bibb lettuce
12 to 20 walnut halves

salad dressing

1 cup plain yogurt
1 tablespoon orange juice
1 tablespoon lemon juice
1 to 2 tablespoons honey

With a melon baller, scoop out round honeydew melon balls.

Cut away skins of oranges, removing the white membrane; slice into ¼-inch slices.

Halve grapes; remove seeds.

Line serving bowl with lettuce leaves, arrange fruits attractively on top, and garnish with walnuts.

Combine dressing ingredients and pour over salad. Serve at once.

fruit and walnut salad

colorful tuna and cheese salad

Yield: 4 servings

8 ounces Gouda cheese,
    cut into ½-inch cubes
1 6½-ounce can tuna, well-drained and
    broken into bite-size pieces
½ cup cold, cooked green beans

2 medium dill pickles, cubed
1 onion, chopped
3 hard-cooked eggs, cubed
1 red pepper (ripe green pepper)
2 small tomatoes, cubed

salad dressing

1 cup plain yogurt
4 tablespoons mayonnaise
2 teaspoons prepared mustard
1 teaspoon sugar

Lettuce leaves

1 teaspoon chopped fresh dill
    (or ½ teaspoon dried dillweed)
1 tablespoon chopped fresh
    parsley leaves
Salt and pepper to taste

In a large bowl combine cheese, tuna, beans, pickles, onion, eggs, pepper, and tomatoes.

Combine and whisk together the dressing ingredients. Pour over salad ingredients; toss lightly. Chill 15 to 20 minutes to blend flavors before serving.

Line serving bowl with lettuce leaves. Arrange salad on top.

colorful tuna and cheese salad

tossed luncheon salad

Yield: About 4 servings

    8 ounces lean cooked leftover beef, cut into julienne strips
    4 ounces cooked ham, chicken, or turkey, cut into julienne strips
    1 large dill pickle, chopped
    1 tart apple, cored and diced
    $\frac{1}{2}$ cup cooked or canned peas, chilled
    $\frac{1}{2}$ cup cooked cauliflower, cut into florets and chilled

salad dressing

    1 cup plain yogurt
    1 tablespoon chopped fresh parsley
    1 tablespoon chopped chives or thinly sliced scallion
    $\frac{1}{2}$ teaspoon paprika
    $\frac{1}{8}$ teaspoon nutmeg
    Salt and pepper to taste

    Lettuce leaves
    1 or 2 hard-cooked eggs, cut into wedges or slices

Combine meats, pickles, apple, and vegetables, except the lettuce.

Blend together the dressing ingredients; pour over meat and vegetables. Toss lightly.

Serve salad on a bed of lettuce leaves. Garnish with hard-cooked egg slices or wedges.

63

herring salad

Yield: 4 to 6 servings

1 cup sour cream
½ cup plain yogurt
1 tablespoon lemon juice
Pinch sugar
2 medium onions, thinly sliced

2 tart apples, cut into thin slices
1 tablespoon chopped fresh dill or
 1 teaspoon dried dillweed
2 8-ounce jars pickled herring, drained and
 cut into bite-size pieces

Combine sour cream, yogurt, lemon juice, sugar, sliced onions that have been separated into rings, apples, and dill.

Alternate herring and sour-cream mixture in layers in a casserole dish. Cover; refrigerate 5 hours. Serve very cold.

herring salad

herring salad with sour cream

dutch herring salad

Yield: 4 servings

 1 small head chicory or lettuce, coarsely shredded
 4 medium new potatoes, boiled, peeled, chilled, and cut into bite-size cubes
 4 ounces cold pickled herring, cut into bite-size pieces
 1 medium onion, coarsely grated
 1 tablespoon vinegar
 2 tablespoons vegetable oil
 ½ teaspoon sugar
 Dash freshly ground black pepper
 1 tablespoon minced parsley
 1 tablespoon minced chives
 1 tablespoon minced dill
 ⅓ cup plain yogurt

In a large salad bowl, combine chicory, potatoes, and herring.
Blend onion, vinegar, oil, sugar, and pepper. Pour over salad ingredients. Toss gently.
Stir herbs into yogurt; pour over salad. Serve at once.

stuffed tomatoes

Yield: 4 servings

 4 large, ripe tomatoes
 1 tablespoon vegetable oil
 1 teaspoon vinegar
 1 teaspoon Worcestershire sauce
 Salt and pepper

tuna filling

 1 6½-ounce can tuna, well-drained
 4 anchovy fillets, coarsely chopped
 2 hard-cooked eggs, chopped
 1 teaspoon capers
 2 tablespoons chopped fresh parsley leaves

 Few blades chives, chopped
 2 tablespoons mayonnaise
 ½ cup plain yogurt
 1 tablespoon lemon juice
 ½ teaspoon celery salt

Cut off the top and scoop out the seeds and pulp from each tomato.
Combine oil, vinegar, Worcestershire sauce, salt, and pepper. Brush the inside of each tomato with the mixture. Let stand 1 hour.
Combine filling ingredients. Mix lightly.
Drain tomatoes; fill with tuna mixture. Serve at once on lettuce.

dutch herring salad

cranberry holiday mold

Try this at Thanksgiving.

Yield: 6 to 8 servings

1 3-ounce package strawberry- or cherry-flavored gelatin dessert
¾ cup boiling water
1 14-ounce jar cranberry orange relish
½ cup chopped walnuts
2 tablespoons lemon juice
2 teaspoons grated orange rind
1 envelope unflavored gelatin
¾ cup cold water
1 8-ounce package cream cheese
1 cup plain yogurt
3 to 4 tablespoons sugar

Dissolve flavored gelatin in boiling water. Add relish, walnuts, lemon juice, and grated rind. Pour into a 1½-quart mold; chill until thickened, about 2 to 3 hours.

Sprinkle unflavored gelatin over cold water in a saucepan; heat over moderate heat, stirring constantly, until gelatin is dissolved. Cool to room temperature.

Beat cream cheese until light and fluffy. Blend in yogurt, sugar, and cooled unflavored-gelatin mixture.

Spoon cream-cheese mixture over the thickened gelatin in the mold. Cover; chill until set, preferably overnight.

Invert mold on a bed of lettuce to serve.

salad dressings

salad dressings

Many of the salad recipes in the preceding section are featured with interesting dressing recipes. Here are some additional ones to serve with your own versions of fruit or vegetable salads.

anchovy salad dressing

Yield: About 1 cup

>1 cup plain yogurt
>3 anchovy fillets
>1 teaspoon paprika
>¼ teaspoon dry mustard
>Salt to taste

Combine all ingredients in a blender jar. Blend until smooth.

avocado salad dressing

Yield: About 2½ cups

>1 large avocado, peeled and pitted
>2 tablespoons fresh lemon juice
>1 cup mayonnaise
>1 cup plain yogurt
>1 very small onion, minced
>1 tablespoon sugar
>1 tablespoon (or less) Worcestershire sauce
>½ teaspoon garlic salt
>Dash Tabasco sauce

Mash avocado with lemon juice. Add all remaining ingredients; blend well. (Ingredients may be blended in a food processor or electric blender.) Chill well before serving. May be kept in the refirgerator for several days if tightly covered.

yogurt mayonnaise

Yield: About 1¼ cups

1 cup plain yogurt
1 tablespoon prepared mustard
2 teaspoons lemon juice
1 teaspoon minced onion
1 tablespoon fresh parsley leaves
¼ teaspoon basil
1 drop Tabasco sauce
Salt to taste
3 tablespoons vegetable oil

Combine all ingredients, except vegetable oil, in a blender jar. Add oil slowly while blending at moderate speed. Use as a salad dressing, not as a spread on sandwiches.

herb salad dressing

Yield: About ½ cup

½ cup plain yogurt
1 tablespoon finely chopped parsley
1 tablespoon finely chopped dill
1 tablespoon finely chopped chives
1 teaspoon lemon juice
2 teaspoons prepared mustard
Pinch garlic powder
Salt and white pepper to taste

Blend together the yogurt, herbs, lemon juice, and mustard. Season to taste with garlic powder, salt, and pepper.
Serve with beef, lamb, salads, or sliced tomatoes and cucumbers.

poppy-seed salad dressing

Celery seeds can be substituted for poppy seeds.

Yield: 1½ cups

1 cup plain yogurt
½ cup coarsely shredded cucumbers
½ cup coarsely shredded radishes
2 tablespoons very thin scallion slices
1 teaspoon poppy seeds
½ teaspoon salt

Combine all ingredients. Serve poured over a tossed salad.

blue-cheese salad dressing

Just right for tossed greens and croutons.

Yield: About 1¼ cups

> 1 cup plain yogurt
> ¼ cup crumbled blue cheese
> ¼ teaspoon garlic salt
> 2 slices crisp bacon, crumbled (or 1 or 2 tablespoons imitation bacon bits)

Combine all ingredients; chill 15 minutes before using. If imitation bacon bits are used, these should be stirred in just before serving to retain their crispness.

garlic–onion salad dressing

Yield: About 1¼ cups

> 1 cup plain yogurt
> 1 medium onion, finely chopped
> 1 clove garlic, minced
> 1 teaspoon paprika
> ¼ teaspoon dry mustard
> ½ teaspoon salt
> 1 tablespoon lemon juice (optional)

Combine all ingredients. Refrigerate at least 15 minutes before using.

lemon–garlic salad dressing

Yield: 1¼ cups

> 1 cup plain yogurt
> 1 tablespoon lemon juice
> 1 clove garlic, crushed or minced
> 1 tablespoon chopped fresh parsley leaves
> ½ teaspoon salt
> ½ teaspoon freshly ground black pepper
> ½ teaspoon grated lemon rind (optional)

Combine all ingredients. Serve with tossed salads.

lemon and honey fruit-salad dressing

So easy to make and enjoy.

Yield: About 1¼ cups

1 cup plain yogurt
1 tablespoon lemon juice
2 tablespoons honey

Combine all ingredients. Serve over a fresh-fruit salad.

pineapple fruit-salad dressing

Yield: About 1¼ cups

1 cup plain yogurt
⅓ cup crushed pineapple, well-drained
2 tablespoons honey

Combine all ingredients; refrigerate unless used immediately.
Serve over a mixed-fruit salad on a bed of greens.

strawberry fruit-salad dressing

Yield: 1¼ cups

1 cup plain yogurt
1 tablespoon honey
¼ cup chopped fresh strawberries
2 tablespoons chopped walnuts or pecans

Combine all ingredients. Serve over your favorite fruit salad.

main dishes and vegetables

hungarian beef goulash

Yield: 4 or 5 servings

> 1½ pounds lean beef (chuck or round), cut into 1-inch cubes
> 2 tablespoons vegetable oil
> 2 medium onions, chopped
> ½ teaspoon salt
> 2 tablespoons paprika
> 1 cup beef broth
> 2 green peppers, cubed
> 2 red peppers (ripe green peppers), cubed
> ½ cup plain yogurt mixed until smooth with 1 tablespoon all-purpose flour

Brown the beef cubes on all sides in hot vegetable oil in a large skillet. Add onions, salt, paprika, and broth. Cover; simmer gently for about 2 hours or until meat is very tender.

Add peppers the last 10 minutes of cooking. Remove lid so most of the cooking liquid can evaporate.

Add yogurt; stir only to distribute it lightly. Serve at once.

beef paprika

Prepare this dish quickly and easily in a covered skillet or cook it in a slow cooker.

Yield: 6 to 8 servings

> 2 to 3 pounds lean beef (chuck or round),
>   cut into 1-inch cubes
> 2 tablespoons vegetable oil
> ¼ cup water
> 1 6-ounce can tomato paste
> 2 cloves garlic
>
> 1½ tablespoons paprika
> 1 teaspoon salt
> 2 green peppers,
>   cut into 1-inch cubes
> 1 cup plain yogurt

Brown beef in hot oil in a large skillet. Add water; stir to pick up the browned bits. Add tomato paste, garlic, paprika, and salt. Cover and simmer over very low heat for 2 hours or pour into a slow cooker and cook on low for about 8 hours.

Add green peppers the last 10 minutes of cooking.

Just before serving, blend yogurt into the thick sauce only until partially mixed. Do not reheat or blend well, or yogurt may curdle. Serve at once.

hungarian beef goulash

beef stroganoff

Yield: 5 or 6 servings

 ½ pound fresh mushrooms, sliced
 1 onion, thinly sliced
 3 tablespoons butter or margarine
 1½ pounds lean beef top of the round steak,
 cut into very thin strips
 ¼ cup all-purpose flour
 1 cup plain yogurt
 1 can condensed consommé
 3 tablespoons tomato paste
 1 teaspoon Worcestershire sauce
 1 teaspoon salt
 ¼ cup sliced black olives (optional)
 ⅓ cup dry sherry

Brown mushrooms and onion in butter in a large skillet. Remove and set aside. Add beef to skillet; brown well.

Combine flour and yogurt. Mix until smooth. Add to beef in skillet along with the undiluted consommé, tomato paste, Worcestershire sauce, and salt. Heat and stir until mixture comes to a boil and is thickened. Stir in the mushroom–onion mixture, olives, and sherry. Heat briefly.

Serve beef at once with mashed potatoes, rice, or noodles.

italian marinated chicken

Yield: 4 servings

 1 2- to 3-pound frying chicken, cut up
 1 cup plain yogurt
 2 tablespoons olive oil
 1 teaspoon vinegar or lemon juice
 1 clove garlic, minced
 1 teaspoon oregano
 1 teaspoon paprika
 1 teaspoon salt

Place chicken pieces in a shallow dish.

Combine remaining ingredients; pour over chicken. Cover and marinate in the refrigerator 3 to 5 hours.

Broil about 5 inches from the heat 15 to 20 minutes on each side. Baste occasionally with marinade.

chicken tarragon

For a simpler version, top baked chicken pieces with Tarragon Sauce (see Index).

Yield: 4 servings

1 2- to 3-pound frying chicken, cut up
2 tablespoons melted butter or margarine
1 teaspoon garlic salt
1 teaspoon tarragon
Dash freshly ground black pepper
1 tablespoon dried parsley leaves

3 tablespoons vinegar
1 tablespoon cornstarch mixed
   with ¼ cup cold water
¾ cup plain yogurt
Salt to taste

Remove the skins from the chicken pieces. Arrange chicken meat-side-up in a large casserole dish. Brush with butter.

Combine garlic salt, tarragon, pepper, and parsley. Sprinkle over buttered chicken. Cover; bake at 350°F for ½ hour. Uncover, add vinegar, and continue baking at 400°F until chicken is golden brown, about 15 to 20 minutes.

Arrange chicken on a warm platter. Drain off accumulated fat, but leave browned drippings and juice. Add cornstarch–water mixture. Heat until thickened. Remove from heat. Stir in yogurt and salt to taste. Pour over chicken.

chicken enchiladas

A Mexican* dish too good to miss!

Yield: 3 or 4 servings

8 corn tortillas

chicken filling

2 cups diced cooked chicken
2 ounces mozzarella cheese, cubed
¼ cup coarsely chopped black olives
½ cup plain yogurt
½ teaspoon salt

enchilada sauce

1 8-ounce can mild
   enchilada sauce
1 8-ounce can tomato sauce

garnish

2 ounces mozzarella cheese, shredded

Combine the filling ingredients. Place some of the filling down the center of each tortilla. Roll, and place flap-side-down, side by side, in an 8 x 8 x 2-inch baking dish.

Combine enchilada and tomato sauces and pour over the tortillas. Be sure to moisten the edges of the tortillas so they do not dry out during baking.

Top with the shredded cheese. Bake at 350°F for 20 minutes or until heated through. Serve at once.

*Yogurt may also be served as a topping on many other Mexican dishes: chalupas, tacos, etc.

lamb with caper sauce

Yield: 6 servings

1 2½- to 3-pound leg of lamb, boned

marinade

1 medium onion, grated
2 tablespoons lemon juice
½ cup wine vinegar
1 cup water
½ teaspoon salt
2 cloves garlic, minced
1 bay leaf, crumbled
4 whole cloves
2 tablespoons chopped fresh parsley
2 tablespoons chopped fresh dill (or 1 tablespoon dried)

cooking broth

5 to 6 cups water
1 carrot, diced
1 stalk celery with leaves, diced
3 sprigs parsley
1 onion, peeled and quartered
1 bay leaf

caper sauce

2 tablespoons butter or margarine
2 tablespoons all-purpose flour
1 cup cooking broth
½ cup plain yogurt
Salt and pepper to taste
2 tablespoons capers
2 tablespoons chopped fresh parsley leaves

Trim excess fat and skin from leg of lamb, if necessary.

Combine ingredients for Marinade in a large, shallow casserole dish. Place lamb in Marinade, cover with plastic wrap, and marinate in the refrigerator 24 hours. Turn meat in the Marinade occasionally.

Remove lamb from marinade and place in a large kettle. Add the ingredients for the Cooking Broth. Water should barely cover the meat. Bring to a boil; simmer gently, covered, for 1½ to 2 hours. Remove meat to a warm platter. Strain and set aside 1 cup of the Cooking Broth to use in the Caper Sauce.

Prepare the Caper Sauce. Melt butter in a skillet and stir in the flour to form a smooth paste. Add reserved broth slowly, stirring constantly. Continue to heat until sauce boils and is thickened. Blend in yogurt, salt and pepper, capers, and parsley. Reheat briefly, but do not boil.

Slice lamb and cover it with some sauce. Serve at once with oven-fried potatoes. Serve remaining sauce separately.

lamb with caper sauce

greek lamb and pilaf casserole

Yield: 4 servings

2 lamb shanks, well-trimmed of all fat
2 tablespoons vegetable oil
1 medium onion, chopped
2½ cups water
1 6-ounce can tomato paste
2 teaspoons whole allspice

½ stick cinnamon
½ teaspoon black peppercorns
1 teaspoon salt
2 tablespoons butter
1 cup uncooked long-grain white rice
1 cup plain yogurt, lightly salted

Brown lamb shanks on all sides in hot oil in a large skillet. Add onion, water, tomato paste, spices, and salt. Cover; simmer for about 1½ hours.

Melt butter in another skillet; brown the rice, stirring constantly, over moderate heat. Set aside.

Measure the lamb cooking broth and add enough additional water to make 2½ cups. Return to lamb after removing and discarding the whole spices. Add the browned rice, cover, and continue cooking another 30 minutes over low heat until rice is tender.

Serve on a large platter. Pass rice separately.

Yogurt should be served in a small bowl as an accompaniment and may be spooned over the lamb and rice, if desired.

albanian lamb stew

albanian lamb stew

Lean beef, chuck or round, may be substituted for the lamb in this recipe to reduce costs. Individual ramekins may be used in the place of a single casserole dish.

Yield: 4 servings

> 1 pound lean lamb, cut into ¾-inch cubes
>   (boneless shoulder or leg of lamb
>   may be used)
> 2 tablespoons vegetable oil
> 1 cup water
> 2 eggs
> 1 cup plain yogurt
> ½ teaspoon salt

Brown cubed lamb in hot vegetable oil in a large skillet. Add water; simmer, uncovered, until the water has evaporated, about 20 to 25 minutes.

Place browned cubes in a greased, shallow, 1-quart casserole dish.

Beat together the eggs, yogurt, and salt. Pour over meat. Bake at 350°F for 20 minutes or until golden brown.

Serve stew at once with a tossed salad containing black olives, lettuce, onions, tomatoes, and perhaps some feta cheese.

schnitzel with ham and caper sauce

Yield: 4 servings

> 4 pork loin chops, about 1 inch thick, bone removed
> 2 tablespoons lemon juice
> Salt and pepper
> 2 tablespoons vegetable oil

ham and caper sauce

> 1 tablespoon fat
> 1 tablespoon all-purpose flour
> 1 cup plain yogurt
> 4 ounces cooked ham (optional), cut into julienne strips
> 1 or 2 medium-size dill pickles, cut into small cubes
> 1 tablespoon capers

Brush pork chops with lemon juice; season with salt and pepper. Let stand 5 to 10 minutes. Pat dry; brown in vegetable oil in a large skillet. Remove to a warm platter.

Drain all but 1 tablespoon of fat from skillet. Add flour to remaining fat; stir to form a smooth paste. Add yogurt; stir to blend and pick up the browned bits. Stir in ham, pickles, and capers. Heat until thickened, stirring constantly.

Spoon sauce over pork chops. Serve at once.

schnitzel with ham and caper sauce

fish with herb sauce

Yield: 4 servings

1½ pounds fresh fish fillets
1 to 2 tablespoons lemon juice
4 tomatoes, peeled and sliced

Salt and pepper
1 strip lean bacon, diced
1 small onion, chopped

herb sauce

½ cup plain yogurt
1 tablespoon all-purpose flour
1 tablespoon chopped parsley leaves
1 tablespoon chopped chives or
    thinly sliced scallions

1 teaspoon dried dillweed (optional)
½ teaspoon tarragon
½ teaspoon chervil

1 tablespoon dried bread crumbs

Sprinkle lemon juice over fish; set aside.

Line the bottom of a greased, shallow casserole dish with the tomato slices. Season with salt and pepper.

In a small skillet combine bacon and onion. Cook until onion is golden.

Combine yogurt, flour, and herbs. Season to taste with salt and pepper.

Place fish fillets on top of tomatoes, pour Herb Sauce over fish, cover with bacon–onion mixture, and sprinkle bread crumbs over all. Cover; bake at 350°F for about 20 minutes or until fish can be separated into flakes with a fork. Serve at once.

Herb Sauce may be reserved and used as a topping after the fish has been baked. Should you choose this method, omit the flour.

fish with herb sauce

baked fish with cucumber sauce

Yield: 4 servings

    1 to 1½ pounds fish fillets
    Fresh parsley leaves (for garnish)

cucumber sauce

    ½ cucumber, peeled, seeded, and coarsely grated
    ½ teaspoon salt
    1 cup plain yogurt
    1 teaspoon chopped fresh dillweed
    ¼ teaspoon freshly ground black pepper

Prepare sauce. Sprinkle grated cucumber with salt; let stand 20 minutes to withdraw some of the water present. Drain away accumulated water; combine cucumber with remaining ingredients.

Place fish on a lightly greased baking sheet. Bake at 425°F for 10 minutes for each inch of thickness or until fish can be separated into flakes with a fork.

Place fish on a warm platter. Ladle sauce over fish; garnish with fresh parsley leaves.

pickled-herring platter

Serve yogurt in place of the more commonly used sour cream with pickled fish.

Yield: 3 or 4 servings

    12 to 16 ounces chilled pickled herring
    1 tablespoon vinegar (optional)
    1 onion, sliced thinly
    ½ cup plain yogurt
    2 cups cooked green beans
    12 small new potatoes, boiled
    2 tablespoons melted butter
    Chopped fresh parsley leaves

Rinse herring with cold water. Arrange on a serving platter. Sprinkle with vinegar, if you like.

Separate onion slices into rings; arrange over herring. Top with yogurt.

Place hot green beans and potatoes on platter with herring. Top vegetables with melted butter and parsley. Serve at once.

Picture on next pages: pickled-herring platter

fillet of flounder with clam and mushroom sauce

Yield: 4 servings

4 flounder fillets, 6 ounces each
Butter or margarine

clam and mushroom sauce

3 tablespoons butter or margarine
3 tablespoons all-purpose flour
1½ cups plain yogurt
1 8-ounce can minced clams, undrained
½ cup mushrooms, sautéed in butter
Salt and freshly ground black pepper to taste

Fresh dill leaves

Sauté flounder in butter or margarine in a large skillet until fish can be separated into flakes with a fork.

Prepare sauce. Melt butter in a saucepan. Add flour; stir to form a smooth paste. Add yogurt; heat and stir over moderate heat just until mixture comes to a boil and is thickened. Add clams, mushrooms, and salt and pepper. Reheat briefly.

Place fish on a warm serving platter. Ladle sauce over fish. Serve at once garnished with sprigs of dill leaves.

good yogurt gravy

Stirred into thickened hot mixtures, yogurt will not curdle. Do not add yogurt directly to a hot pan or stir into thin liquids. Yogurt added to gravies gives them an interesting tang. Do not overheat gravy or yogurt may curdle.

Yield: 1½ cups

2 tablespoons fat from pan drippings
2 tablespoons all-purpose flour
1 cup water or drippings with fat removed
½ cup plain yogurt
Salt and pepper to taste

Pour off accumulated drippings from cooked meat or poultry. Skim off 2 tablespoons fat and return to pan. Stir in flour to form a smooth paste. Add 1 cup drippings or water; stir to combine with flour mixture and pick up the browned bits in the pan. Heat and stir until mixture boils and is thickened. Remove from heat; stir in yogurt. Season to taste. Serve at once.

Yogurt may be added to a canned, prepared gravy after heating.

vegetable stew with lobster

vegetable stew with lobster

Yield: 6 servings

 1 10-ounce package frozen cauliflower
 1 10-ounce package frozen baby carrots
 1 10-ounce package frozen white or green asparagus tips
 1 10-ounce package frozen peas
 2 tablespoons butter
 2 tablespoons all-purpose flour
 1½ cups reserved cooking liquid from vegetables
 ¼ teaspoon nutmeg
 Salt and pepper to taste
 4 or 5 ounces canned black Chinese mushrooms, drained
 ½ cup plain yogurt
 8 to 16 ounces cooked lobster meat, cut into bite-size pieces
 Chopped fresh parsley leaves

Cook cauliflower, carrots, asparagus, and peas according to package directions. Drain, reserving and combining the cooking liquids.

Melt butter in a large saucepan. Stir in flour to make a smooth paste. Gradually stir in 1½ cups of the reserved vegetable cooking liquids. Continue to heat and stir until mixture comes to a boil and is thickened. Add nutmeg and salt and pepper. Add cooked vegetables and mushrooms; heat through. Just before serving, stir in yogurt.

Garnish stew with lobster and parsley. Serve at once.

new potatoes with herbed cottage–cheese sauce

Yield: 6 to 8 servings

> **2 to 3 pounds small new potatoes**
> **Salt**

herbed cottage-cheese sauce

> **½ cup plain yogurt**
> **1 12-ounce carton cottage cheese, creamed in a blender**
> **1 onion, finely chopped**
> **4 hard-cooked eggs**
> **1 tablespoon lemon juice**
> **Salt and pepper to taste**
> **3 tablespoons chopped chives or thinly sliced scallions**

Scrub potatoes with a soft brush; do not peel. Boil 20 to 30 minutes in salted water, until tender.

Stir yogurt into cottage cheese. Add onion. Strain egg yolks through a sieve, chop egg whites, and add to cottage-cheese mixture. Season with lemon juice and salt and pepper. Stir in chives or scallions. Serve as a sauce with potatoes.

Place cream-cheese mixture in a bowl in the center of a large serving dish or platter. Arrange capers, tomatoes, chives, onion, shrimp, and small dishes of paprika and caraway seeds around it. Serve crackers and snack bread in baskets on the side. Each individual spreads the cheese mixture on a cracker and selects one or more toppings.

fresh cooked vegetables in yogurt sauces

Turn to the section on Sauces and select a favorite one to serve over drained, cooked vegetables.

Avoid topping a warm vegetable with a yogurt sauce that has *not* been thickened with flour, starch, or eggs. The acid and heat from the vegetable will curdle plain yogurt within minutes of its addition to a hot vegetable. The thickened sauces are perfect to use, however!

new potatoes with herbed cottage-cheese sauce

91

potatoes in fresh herb sauce

potatoes in fresh herb sauce

Especially good to make if you have an herb garden.

Yield: 4 servings

2 tablespoons butter or margarine
½ leek, sliced
1 medium onion, diced
2 ounces boiled ham, finely diced
1½ cups beef bouillon
2 tablespoons all-purpose flour mixed
    to a smooth paste with 2
    tablespoons cold water
Salt and pepper to taste

1 tablespoon lemon juice
3 tablespoons chopped fresh parsley
3 tablespoons chopped chives
2 sprigs fresh dill, chopped
2 sprigs fresh tarragon, chopped
1 sprig fresh thyme, chopped
8 to 12 new potatoes, boiled and sliced
½ cup plain yogurt
Sprigs fresh herbs (garnish)

Heat butter in a skillet; add leek, onion, and ham; cook and stir until onions and leek are transparent, about 5 to 7 minutes. Add bouillon and flour–water paste. Heat and stir until mixture boils and is thickened. Season to taste with salt and pepper. Add lemon juice, herbs, and potatoes. Heat through. Stir in yogurt just before serving. Garnish with sprigs of fresh herbs.

quiche

Yield: 1 9- or 10-inch quiche; 4 to 6 servings

Pastry for a 9- or 10-inch pie shell (see Index)
4 ounces shredded Swiss cheese
4 eggs
2 cups plain yogurt
½ teaspoon salt
Dash nutmeg
Dash pepper
Butter or margarine

Line a 9- or 10-inch pie pan or a 10-inch quiche mold with prepared pastry.

Combine cheese, eggs, yogurt, salt, nutmeg, and pepper. Stir until ingredients are well-blended. Pour into prepared shell.

Dot surface with butter or margarine. Bake at 375°F for 30 minutes or until a knife inserted 2 inches in from the edge comes out clean. Do not overbake, or filling may separate. Serve warm with a tossed salad and glasses of wine.

quiche variations

quiche lorraine

Place 4 or 5 strips of cooked bacon, each cut into 3 or 4 pieces, in the pastry shell before adding the cheese mixture.

onion quiche

Sauté 2 sliced onions in butter or margarine until soft. Arrange in the pastry shell before adding the cheese mixture.

seafood quiche

Arrange cooked lobster, scallops, shrimps, or flaked fish in the pastry shell before adding cheese mixture.

other variations

Add one or more of the following:

Sliced mushrooms, sautéed in butter
3 or 4 tablespoons Parmesan cheese
Chopped fresh parsley leaves
Chopped spinach, cooked and drained
Chopped fresh tomatoes
Sliced zucchini, sautéed in butter

open-faced chicken-salad sandwiches

open-faced chicken-salad sandwiches

Yield: 4 servings

> **4 slices toast**
> **½ head Bibb lettuce, thinly sliced**
> **8 to 12 ounces cooked chicken breast meat, cut into thin slices**

dressing

> **⅓ cup plain yogurt (may be part mayonnaise)**
> **1 teaspoon horseradish**
> **1 tablespoon catsup**
> **2 tablespoons orange juice**
> **1 tablespoon brandy**
> **Salt and pepper to taste**

topping

> **2 hard-cooked eggs, sliced or cut into wedges**
> **2 medium tomatoes, sliced**
> **8 canned pineapple chunks**
> **2 maraschino cherries, halved**

Top slices of toast with shredded lettuce. Arrange sliced chicken meat on top. Combine Dressing ingredients; pour over chicken.

Garnish each sandwich with wedges of hard-cooked eggs, tomato slices, pineapple chunks, and half a cherry. Serve at once.

94

tuna garden sandwiches

Yield: 4 sandwiches

  1 7¾-ounce can tuna, well-drained
  ¼ cup grated carrots
  2 tablespoons grated green pepper
  2 tablespoons grated celery
  ½ cup creamed cottage cheese
  ¼ cup plain yogurt
  Salt and pepper to taste
  8 slices bread or toast
  Sliced tomatoes
  Shredded lettuce
  Grated cheese

Combine tuna, vegetables, cottage cheese, yogurt, and seasonings. Chill until ready for use. Spread on bran or whole-wheat bread. Top with lettuce, tomato slices, and a large pinch of grated cheese.

pita sandwiches

Pita bread, the flat Middle-Eastern bread that can be opened into a pocket, is excellent for sandwiches with yogurt toppings. The yogurt topping will stay in place and not soak through the bread.

Yield: Varies

  Pita bread—1 5- or 6-inch bread per person

assorted fillings:

  Cubes of cream cheese
  Cubed cooked chicken
  Chopped hard-cooked eggs
  Slivers of smoked or boiled ham
  Chopped onion
  Small cooked shrimp
  Fresh tomatoes, sliced or cubed
  Cubed cooked turkey
  Chopped walnuts

assorted toppings:

  Shredded cheese
  Finely shredded lettuce
  Sliced green or black olives
  Minced green or red peppers
  Finely sliced scallions or onions

dressings:

  Plain yogurt, lightly salted
  Any of the yogurt salad dressings or dips (see Index)

Slice an edge off each pita bread and open the bread to form a pocket.
On a buffet table arrange bowls of fillings, toppings, and dressings. Allow each guest or family member to assemble his own sandwich. Delicious as a midnight buffet! Serve with assorted scented or spiced hot teas.

sauces

mock bearnaise sauce

An awfully good lower calorie substitute for the "real thing" (which is usually made from a full cup of butter).

Yield: 1½ cups

> 2 tablespoons dry white wine
> 1 tablespoon vinegar
> 1 teaspoon tarragon
> 2 teaspoons minced onion
> 3 tablespoons butter
> ½ teaspoon salt
> 1 cup plain yogurt
> 2 eggs

Combine wine, vinegar, tarragon, and onion in a saucepan. Bring to a boil; reduce to 1 tablespoon. Stir in butter and salt. Remove from heat.

Whisk together yogurt and eggs. Add to butter mixture in saucepan. Heat, whisking constantly, over moderate heat just until mixture barely begins to boil. Do not overheat, or mixture will curdle. Serve warm or chilled over omelets, steaks, or vegetables.

mock hollandaise sauce

Another tasty lower calorie version of the "real thing," usually made with melted butter.

Yield: 1½ cups

> 2 tablespoons lemon juice
> 3 tablespoons melted butter
> 1 cup plain yogurt
> ½ teaspoon salt
> 2 eggs

Whisk together all ingredients in a saucepan. Heat, whisking constantly, over moderate heat until mixture barely begins to boil. Remove at once.

Serve warm or chilled over well-drained broccoli, asparagus, or other vegetables, or serve over omelets or sliced roast beef.

tomato–horseradish sauce

A perfect partner for beef dishes.

Yield: About ⅓ cup

¼ cup plain yogurt
2 tablespoons catsup
1 teaspoon horseradish
1 tablespoon freshly chopped parsley leaves

Combine all ingredients. Serve over hamburgers or as a dip for beef fondue.

medium white sauce

Use in recipes for creamed and scalloped dishes.

Yield: 1 cup

2 tablespoons butter or margarine
2 tablespoons all-purpose flour
1 cup plain yogurt
½ teaspoon salt

Melt butter in a saucepan. Stir in flour until smooth. Remove from heat; gradually stir in yogurt. Add salt. Heat over moderate heat until sauce boils, stirring constantly.

thin white sauce

Use as a basis for cream soups and in other recipes calling for a thin white sauce.

Yield: 1 cup

1 tablespoon butter or margarine
1 tablespoon all-purpose flour
1 cup plain yogurt
½ teaspoon salt

Follow recipe directions for Medium White Sauce.

piquant sauce

Yield: ¾ cup

½ cup plain yogurt (may be part mayonnaise)
2 tablespoons applesauce
2 tablespoons prepared horseradish
1 teaspoon lemon juice
Salt and white pepper to taste
¼ teaspoon sugar

Combine first 4 ingredients; stir until blended. Season to taste with salt, pepper, and sugar.

Serve with meats or as a dip for vegetables.

horseradish sauce

Yield: ¾ cup

½ cup plain yogurt (may be part mayonnaise)
3 tablespoons prepared horseradish
1 tablespoon orange juice
Salt and white pepper to taste
¼ teaspoon sugar

Blend thoroughly the first 3 ingredients. Season to taste with salt, pepper, and sugar.

Serve with beef or seafood.

lemon–parsley vegetable sauce

Yield: About ½ cup

1 egg
½ cup plain yogurt
2 teaspoons lemon juice
1 tablespoon chopped fresh parsley leaves

Place all ingredients in the top of a double boiler. Heat over simmering water, stirring constantly until thickened. Do not overheat, or mixture will curdle.

Serve over well-drained broccoli, asparagus, green beans, or another favorite vegetable.

Picture on opposite page, top to bottom: piquant sauce, horseradish sauce, herb salad dressing

tartar sauce

Yield: About 1 cup

⅓ cup yogurt
⅓ cup mayonnaise
1 tablespoon minced onion or scallion
1 tablespoon capers

2 tablespoons pickle relish
1 tablespoon minced green pepper
2 teaspoons minced fresh parsley
  leaves

Combine all ingredients. Serve chilled with baked or broiled fish or as a dip for cold vegetables.

curry sauce

Yield: About 1¼ cups

1 cup plain yogurt
1 teaspoon curry powder
¼ teaspoon dry mustard

¼ teaspoon lemon peel
2 teaspoons lemon juice
Salt to taste

Combine all ingredients. Serve cold with meats, fish, or cold cuts.

cheese sauce

Yield: About 1¼ cups

½ cup grated cheese (cheddar, blue, Jack, etc.)
1 cup Thin White Sauce (see Index)

Add cheese and garlic powder to hot white sauce. Stir over low heat just until blended. Serve hot over vegetables.

newburg sauce

Yield: About 1⅓ cups

1 cup Medium White Sauce (see Index)
1 egg yolk

¼ cup dry sherry
Few grains cayenne

Prepare Yogurt Sauce according to recipe directions. Stir a little of the hot mixture into the egg yolk; return this to the hot sauce. Stir over very low heat for about 1 minute. Stir in sherry and cayenne.
Serve with scallops, lobster, or other seafood.

mexican topping

Use this to top tacos or chalupas.

Yield: About 1¼ cups

> 1 cup plain yogurt
> 2 teaspoons chopped roasted, peeled chilies
>   (available canned in the Mexican
>   food section of your supermarket)
> ½ cup diced very ripe tomatoes
> 1 teaspoon chili powder
> Garlic salt to taste
> Grated Monterey Jack cheese (optional)

Combine all ingredients. Chill; serve in a small bowl.

tomato sauce

Yield: About 1½ cups

> 1 cup yogurt
> 1 teaspoon oregano
> 2 tablespoons dry white or red wine
> ½ tomato, peeled and finely diced
> ¼ teaspoon freshly ground black pepper
> ½ teaspoon salt
> 2 tablespoons olive oil

Combine all ingredients. Serve with cold cuts, beef fondue, or over salad greens.

mustard sauce

Excellent as a sauce for cold, sliced cooked meats at a buffet. Use less dry mustard for a milder flavor.

Yield: About 1¾ cups

> ⅓ cup mayonnaise
> ½ cup prepared mustard
> ⅔ cup plain yogurt
> ½ teaspoon dry mustard
> 1 tablespoon minced parsley leaves
> 2 hard-cooked eggs, chopped
> 1 teaspoon lemon juice
> Salt to taste

Combine all ingredients; chill for 20 to 30 minutes before serving.

remoulade sauce

The tangy flavor is especially good with sweet, ripe tomatoes or as an accompaniment to hamburgers or steak. Serve as a topping for your own version of a hamburger in a bun.

Yield: 1 cup

> 1 cup plain yogurt
> 2 hard-cooked eggs, chopped
> 1 tablespoon chopped capers
> 2 tablespoons chopped fresh parsley leaves
> 1½ teaspoons dry mustard
> ½ teaspoon tarragon
> ⅓ teaspoon garlic salt

Combine all ingredients. Chill well before serving. Keeps several days in the refrigerator.

sweet-and-sour sauce

Yield: About 2 cups

> 2 eggs
> ¼ cup lemon juice
> ½ cup honey
> 1 teaspoon grated lemon peel
> 1 tablespoon poppy seeds
> 1 cup plain yogurt
> Salt to taste

In the top of a double boiler whisk together eggs, lemon juice, and honey. Heat, stirring constantly, over simmering water until thickened. Stir in lemon peel and poppy seeds. Cool. Stir in yogurt and salt. Chill or serve warm. Good with poultry or vegetables.

tarragon sauce

A luscious sauce, especially good with hot or cold chicken.

Yield: About ½ cup

> ½ cup plain yogurt
> 1 tablespoon tarragon
> 2 teaspoons lemon juice
> ½ teaspoon salt

Combine all ingredients. Serve with hot baked or broiled chicken or turkey slices.

frozen yogurt

frozen yogurt

A frozen dessert consists of very small ice crystals and bubbles of air embedded in a sugar solution. When the ice crystals are very small, the frozen dessert is smooth and velvety. Air bubbles contribute to a light texture.

To keep the crystals small, the mixture must be agitated while it is freezing. Frozen yogurt simply is not sweetened, flavored yogurt that has been popped in the freezer and frozen until firm. If you have tried this method, you soon learned it became so hard that inserting a spoon into it was impossible once it was solidly frozen.

To make frozen yogurt with the texture of ice cream, you really must use an ice cream maker—either an inexpensive hand-operated model or an electrically operated model. Place the mixture in the metal can, insert the dashers, set the can in the bucket, and use the correct proportions of crushed ice and salt. The mixture is cranked to break up ice crystals as they form and to incorporate air. The entire procedure takes only 10 to 15 minutes. In short, follow the directions the manufacturer has provided with the ice-cream maker. Fresh from the ice-cream maker, the mixture has the delightful consistency of soft-serve ice cream. It can be packed in containers and refrozen until firmer in the freezer section of your refrigerator. Most people prefer to eat it immediately.

If you do not have an ice-cream maker, you can make frozen yogurt popsicles. Here, you do want a solid, firm product, not one with the consistency of ice cream. Spoon sweetened, flavored yogurt into popsicle molds, and freeze. They're surprisingly good. My children—and all their friends—find them irresistible.

Another alternative for those who do not have an ice-cream maker but still wish to prepare frozen yogurt, is to select a recipe for a still-frozen dessert. These are frozen in a metal tray in the freezing compartment of the refrigerator.

To prevent such desserts from becoming rock-hard in the freezer, they must be beaten once or twice when partially frozen. A meringue or whipped-cream base is usually folded in to incorporate the air so necessary for a light, soft dessert. In addition, they should be removed from the freezer 10 minutes prior to serving, to soften them.

vanilla frozen yogurt I

Very easy to prepare in a hand-cranked or in an electric ice-cream maker. Absolutely delicious!! Be sure to try some of the suggested variations.

When made from 2% milk, this recipe furnishes about 750 calories or about 125 calories per cup.

Yield: About 1½ quarts

> ½ **cup sugar**
> **2 teaspoons vanilla**
> **Dash salt**
> **3 cups plain yogurt***

Add sugar, vanilla, and salt to yogurt. Stir well. Freeze in an ice-cream maker (using 1 cup rock salt for each gallon of crushed ice) according to the manufacturer's instructions.

---

*For a smoother texture (very small ice-crystal formation) use Thickened Yogurt (see Index), which contains gelatin. A commercial yogurt with gelatin already added (see its label for statement of ingredients) may also be used.

vanilla frozen yogurt II

The gelatin is recommended only because its use will result in a slightly smoother product. The dissolved gelatin interferes with the formation of large ice crystals during freezing and causes very tiny ones to form. The result is a very fine-textured frozen dessert. Gelatin also thickens the mixture and enables more air to be incorporated during cranking.

Yield: About 1½ quarts

> **2 teaspoons unflavored gleatin**
> ½ **cup milk**
> ½ **cup sugar**
> **Dash salt**
> **3 cups plain yogurt**
> **1 teaspoon vanilla**

Soften gelatin in milk; heat over low heat, stirring constantly, until gelatin is completely dispersed. Add sugar and salt. Stir well. Cool to room temperature.

Add yogurt and vanilla to gelatin mixture; freeze in an ice-cream maker (using 1 cup rock salt for each gallon of crushed ice) according to the manufacturer's instructions.

peach frozen yogurt

Yield: About 1½ quarts

Omit the vanilla from Vanilla Frozen Yogurt I or II and substitute ½ cup pureed or chopped peaches. Add before freezing, or fold in after cranking is completed, for a rippled effect.

blueberry frozen yogurt

Yield: About 1½ quarts

Substitute ½ cup fresh blueberries for peaches in recipe for Peach Frozen Yogurt.

honey and lemon frozen yogurt

Yield: About 1½ quarts

Substitute ¼ cup lemon juice and ¼ cup honey for peaches in recipe for Peach Frozen Yogurt.

maple frozen yogurt

Yield: About 1½ quarts

Substitute maple flavoring for vanilla in Frozen Vanilla Yogurt I or II.

pineapple frozen yogurt

Yield: About 1½ quarts

Follow recipe for Peach Frozen Yogurt, but substitute ½ cup crushed pineapple.

strawberry frozen yogurt

Yield: About 1½ quarts

Substitute ½ cup crushed strawberries for peaches in recipe for Peach Frozen Yogurt.

strawberry frozen yogurt

A still-frozen dessert; no ice-cream freezer is needed.

Yield: 4 servings

2 teaspoons gelatin
3 tablespoons milk
1 cup plain yogurt
2 tablespoons sugar
1/8 teaspoon salt
5/8 cup sieved frozen strawberries
1½ tablespoons lemon juice
½ cup whipping cream, whipped

Soak gelatin in milk in a custard cup. Set the cup containing the mixture into boiling water; stir until the gelatin is completely dispersed.

Combine yogurt, sugar, and salt. Stir in the gelatin mixture. Stir in the berries and lemon juice. Chill until viscous, then beat until foamy. Fold in the whipped cream.

Pour the mixture into a metal ice-cube tray, cover with foil, and freeze.

blueberry frozen yogurt

A still-frozen dessert.

Yield: 4 servings

1 pint blueberries, washed and small stems completely removed
¼ cup sugar
½ cup light corn syrup
2 cups plain yogurt

Place berries, sugar, and corn syrup in a blender jar; blend until smooth, about 20 seconds. Add yogurt; blend only until combined.

Pour into a metal ice-cube tray, cover with foil, and freeze until firm, but not hard, about 3 hours.

Break up frozen mixture and place in blender jar. Blend until smooth, about 1 minute. Return to metal tray and freeze.

vanilla-fudge frozen yogurt

Yield: 1½ quarts

Vanilla Frozen Yogurt I or II
About ⅓ to ½ cup chocolate syrup

At the completion of cranking, lightly swirl chocolate syrup through frozen yogurt to create a marbled appearance. Serve at once or refreeze to firm.

rum–raisin frozen yogurt

Yield: About 1½ quarts

¾ cup seedless raisins
¼ cup rum
Dash nutmeg
Dash cinnamon
1½ quarts freshly prepared Frozen Vanilla Yogurt I or II

Soak raisins in rum with a dash of cinnamon and nutmeg for about an hour or until raisins are plump. Chill.

Fold rum–raisin mixture gently into freshly prepared Frozen Vanilla Yogurt. Serve at once or refreeze to harden according to the manufacturer's instructions.

butter-pecan frozen yogurt

Yield: 1½ quarts

3 cups plain yogurt	Dash salt
½ cup brown sugar	3 tablespoons butter
2 teaspoons vanilla	½ cup coarsely chopped pecans

Combine yogurt, brown sugar, vanilla, and salt. Stir well and freeze in an ice-cream maker (using 1 cup rock salt for each gallon of crushed ice) according to the manufacturer's directions.

Melt butter in a large skillet; brown the pecans over low heat for 4 to 5 minutes. Cool and gently fold into the freshly prepared frozen mixture. Serve at once or pack in containers and refreeze until firm.

coffee–nut frozen yogurt

A still-frozen dessert.

Yield: 4 servings

2 egg whites	½ cup whipping cream, whipped
⅔ cup sugar	1 cup plain yogurt
1 cup water	½ cup chopped walnuts
1 tablespoon instant coffee, preferably freeze-dried	

Beat the egg whites until stiff.

Combine sugar and water in a saucepan; boil until the syrup reaches 112°F. Add the coffee.

Slowly add the hot syrup to the beaten egg whites while beating constantly. Cover and chill.

Fold in the whipped cream, yogurt, and nuts. Pour into a metal ice-cube tray, cover with foil, and freeze.

cherries jubilee

Yield: 6 to 8 servings

> 3 tablespoons raspberry jam or preserves
> 1 tablespoon butter
> 2 cups canned tart cherries, well-drained
> ½ cup kirsch
> Frozen Vanilla Yogurt I or II

Melt jam over low heat. Add butter; stir until melted. Add cherries; heat through. This step may be done in a chafing dish.

Heat kirsch in a small saucepan. Pour over cherries and ignite. Spoon flaming cherries over frozen yogurt in dessert dishes.

pineapple frozen sherbet

A still-frozen dessert, very refreshing at any time of year.

Yield: 4 servings

> 1 envelope unflavored gelatin
> 3 tablespoons skim milk or water
> 2 cups plain yogurt
> ½ cup sugar
> 1 9-ounce can crushed pineapple, lightly drained
> 1 teaspoon vanilla
> 1 egg white
> 2 tablespoons sugar

Soak gelatin in milk or water in a custard cup. Set cup in boiling water; stir until gelatin is completely dispersed.

Combine yogurt, ½ cup sugar, pineapple, and vanilla. Stir in gelatin mixture. Pour into a metal ice-cube tray, cover with foil, and freeze until firm but not hard, about 3 hours.

Break frozen mixture into chunks; beat until smooth in a blender or with an electric mixer.

Beat egg white until foamy. Gradually add sugar, while beating, until soft peaks form. Fold into beaten yogurt mixture. Return to metal ice-cube tray or a loaf pan. Cover and freeze.

Picture on opposite page: cherries jubilee

avocado frozen yogurt

Easy to prepare, smooth, for avocado afficionados.

Yield: 1 quart

1 to 1½ quarts Frozen Vanilla Yogurt I or II
1 or 2 large very ripe avocados, peeled and pitted

Use freshly prepared Frozen Vanilla Yogurt. If using commercially prepared frozen yogurt, allow to soften slightly at room temperature.

Mash avocado with a fork or puree in a blender until smooth. Immediately blend into the frozen yogurt and return to the freezer to harden before serving.

peppermint-stick frozen yogurt

Yield: About 1½ quarts

3 cups plain yogurt
1 cup crushed peppermint sticks*
2 teaspoons vanilla
Dash salt

Place yogurt, crushed peppermint, vanilla, and salt in the metal can of an ice-cream maker. Freeze according to the manufacturer's instructions, using 1 cup rock salt for each gallon of crushed ice.

*Break into small pieces and blend in blender or crush in a plastic bag by rolling with a rolling pin.

frozen yogurt in a cup

Just like the store-bought kind and perhaps even better!

Yield: Varies

1 recipe freshly prepared Frozen Vanilla Yogurt I or II
6- or 8-ounce size paper cups
Assorted fruit preserves (optional)
Aluminum foil

Scoop freshly cranked frozen vanilla yogurt into paper cups. Top with 1 or 2 tablespoons of your favorite fruit preserves, if you wish. Cover tops snugly with foil; fasten with rubber bands.

Store cups in the freezing compartment of your refrigerator. Let stand at room temperature about 10 minutes to soften slightly before serving.

tropical sherbet

Yield: About 2 quarts

> 4 cups plain yogurt
> ⅓ cup frozen orange juice concentrate (or Hawaiian Punch or frozen pineapple
>   juice concentrate)
> 1 cup sugar
> Dash salt

Stir together all ingredients. Freeze in an ice-cream maker (using 1⅓ cups rock salt for each gallon crushed ice) according to the manufacturer's instructions.

popsicles

Make several of each flavor at one time.

Yield: 2 or 3 popsicles

> 1 cup plain yogurt
> 2 to 3 tablespoons jelly, orange marmalade, jam, or fruit preserves

Whisk together the yogurt and the jelly, marmalade, jam, or preserves. Mixture need not be smooth. Spoon into popsicle molds or into small paper cups with a stick inserted in the center. Freeze and enjoy.

bill's quick popsicles

Yield: 2 or 3 popsicles

> 1 cup commercially prepared fruit-flavored yogurt

Spoon yogurt into popsicle molds and freeze until firm.

orange–vanilla popsicles

Yield: About 6 to 8 popsicles

> 2 cups plain yogurt
> ½ to ¾ cup frozen orange juice concentrate
> 1 to 2 teaspoons vanilla

Combine all ingredients. Pour into popsicle molds and freeze until firm.

vanilla frozen custard I

This recipe was developed especially for use in the Salton® Ice Cream Machine™. The cornstarch and gelatin are necessary for smooth texture and good body in this ice cream, which does not freeze as rapidly as one frozen in an ice and salt mixture.

Yield: 3½ cups (about 100 calories per ½ cup)

> ½ cup sugar
> 1 tablespoon cornstarch
> Dash salt
> 2 cups yogurt
> 2 eggs, beaten
> 1 teaspoon gelatin
> ¼ cup skim milk
> 1¼ teaspoons vanilla

Combine sugar, cornstarch, salt, and 1 cup of the yogurt in a saucepan. Heat slowly, stirring constantly, over low-moderate heat until thickened, about 8 to 10 minutes. Stir a small amount of this hot mixture into the beaten eggs, then stir the egg mixture into the cornstarch mixture. Continue heating, stirring constantly, until thickened, about 4 minutes.

Soften gelatin in skim milk, then add to hot mixture. Stir well and chill.

Add remaining 1 cup of yogurt and vanilla to chilled mixture. Place in metal can of the Salton® Ice Cream Machine™ and freeze according to the manufacturer's directions.

vanilla frozen custard II

A still-frozen dessert.

Yield: 4 servings

> 2 eggs, separated
> ½ cup sugar
> 1 teaspoon vanilla
> 2 cups plain yogurt

Beat egg yolks until light. Add sugar and vanilla; continue beating until sugar is dissolved.

Beat egg whites until stiff. Fold in yolk mixture. Gently fold in yogurt.

Pour into a metal ice-cube tray, cover with foil, and freeze.

frozen lemon torte

A still-frozen dessert.

Yield: 6 servings

¾ cup crushed vanilla wafers
3 egg yolks, beaten
¼ cup lemon juice
1 teaspoon grated lemon rind
½ cup sugar
1½ cups plain yogurt
3 egg whites, beaten until stiff

Lightly butter a metal ice-cube tray. Line with half of the wafer crumbs.

In the top of a double boiler combine beaten yolks, lemon juice and rind, and sugar. Heat over boiling water, stirring occasionally, until thick. Cool.

Add yogurt and beaten egg whites to the cooled lemon mixture. Pour over wafer crumbs in the tray. Top with remaining crumbs.

Cover and freeze. Cut into squares to serve.

frozen lemon mallow

A still-frozen dessert.

Yield: 4 servings

½ cup sugar
6 tablespoons lemon juice
2½ cups diced canned fruit, drained
2 eggs, beaten
¼ teaspoon salt
32 marshmallows, snipped into quarters with kitchen shears
1 cup whipping cream, whipped
1 cup plain yogurt

Combine sugar, 3 tablespoons of the lemon juice, and diced fruit. Chill.

In the top of a double boiler, combine eggs, salt, and the remaining 3 tablespoons of lemon juice. Cook over boiling water, stirring constantly, until thick. Add marshmallows. Stir until melted. Cool.

Fold in chilled fruit mixture, whipping cream, and yogurt.

Pour into a metal ice-cube tray, cover with aluminum foil, and freeze.

desserts and snacks

ambrosia

Yield: 4 to 6 servings

> 1 11-ounce can mandarin orange sections, drained
> 2 apples, cored and diced
> 2 or 3 bananas, sliced
> 1 8-ounce can pineapple tidbits, drained
> 1 cup flaked coconut
> ½ to 1 cup miniature marshmallows
> 1 cup plain yogurt

Combine fruits, coconut, and marshmallows. Chill well. Just before serving, stir in yogurt. Garnish with chopped nuts, if desired.

alpine fruit dessert

Yield: 6 servings

> 2 envelopes unflavored gelatin
> ½ cup orange, pineapple, or apricot juice
> 4 egg yolks
> 1 to 2 tablespoons honey or sugar
> ¼ teaspoon grated lemon rind
> 3 tablespoons lemon juice
> 2 cups coarsely chopped fresh fruit such as strawberries and bananas, blue-
>   berries and strawberries, or apples and raisins
> 2 cups plain yogurt
> 4 egg whites, beaten until stiff

Soften gelatin in fruit juice. Completely dissolve over hot water.

Beat yolks until light. Stir in honey, lemon rind, lemon juice, and fresh fruit. Stir in the gelatin mixture and yogurt. Fold beaten egg whites into the fruit and yogurt mixture.

Spoon into dessert dishes or tall parfait glasses and chill until firm. Garnish with fresh fruit.

blackberry-cream dessert

blackberry-cream dessert

Strictly for those who are not watching their calories, this dessert furnishes about 700 calories a portion.

Yield: 4 servings

1 pound fresh blackberries or raspberries	2 tablespoons vodka
4 ounces cream cheese	2 tablespoons lemon juice
1 cup plain yogurt	2 egg whites
¼ cup honey	2 cups heavy cream
2 egg yolks	16 small macaroons or whole almonds
	16 walnut halves

Set aside 16 berries for a garnish; strain remaining berries through a fine sieve to remove seeds.

Blend strained raspberries with cream cheese, yogurt, honey, egg yolks, vodka, and lemon juice. Stir until smooth and creamy.

Beat egg whites until soft peaks form. Beat cream until stiff. Fold both into raspberry mixture. Spoon into 4 individual dessert dishes. Chill until set.

Just before serving, garnish each with macaroons or almonds, walnut halves, and reserved berries.

115

strawberry-creme dessert

Yield: 3 or 4 servings

1 pint strawberries, cleaned and hulled
¼ cup sugar
2 cups plain yogurt
1 teaspoon vanilla
Grated chocolate
2 tablespoons chopped pistachio nuts
Whipped cream

Reserve several strawberries to use as a garnish. Puree remainder in a blender.

Combine pureed strawberries, sugar, yogurt, and vanilla. Spoon into individual dessert dishes and garnish with chocolate, nuts, and a dab of whipped cream.

strawberry-creme dessert

strawberry–lemon dessert

Yield: 6 servings

> 2 3-ounce packages lemon gelatin dessert
> 1½ cups boiling water
> 1 7-ounce bottle lemon–lime soda
> ¼ cup lemon juice
> Grated rind of 1 lemon
> 2 cups plain yogurt
> 2 cups fresh strawberries, sliced and sweetened to taste with sugar

Combine gelatin and boiling water. Stir to dissolve. Add soda, lemon juice, and rind. Chill until the consistency of egg white, about 2 to 3 hours. Beat until foamy.

Fold in yogurt. Pour into 6 dessert dishes or parfait glasses. Chill until firm. Garnish with fresh strawberries.

cranberry dessert

Yield: 4 servings

> 3 cups yogurt
> ⅓ cup orange juice
> Honey or sugar to taste
> ¼ cup whole cranberry sauce

Blend yogurt, orange juice, and honey until smooth. Stir in cranberry sauce. Serve in individual dessert dishes.

apricot dessert

Yield: 4 servings

> 3 cups yogurt
> 3 tablespoons honey
> 1 tablespoon rum
> 8 canned apricots, sliced

Combine all ingredients. Serve in small dessert bowls.

cherry kirsch dessert

cherry kirsch dessert

Weight watchers, please note. Over 400 calories per serving!

Yield: 4 servings

1 pound fresh cherries, pits removed
½ cup honey
¼ cup kirsch
1 tablespoon lemon juice

2 cups plain yogurt
1 cup whipping cream
1 teaspoon vanilla

Combine cherries with about ⅓ cup of honey, kirsch, and lemon juice. Chill 15 minutes.

Blend yogurt with remaining honey.

Beat cream until stiff. Stir in vanilla. Remove 2 tablespoons of the whipped cream and reserve for use as a garnish. Fold remainder into sweetened yogurt.

Alternate layers of cherries and yogurt–cream mixture in tall parfait glasses. Garnish each with reserved whipped cream. Serve at once.

elfin's dessert

elfin's dessert

Appropriately named, this light dessert contains around 100 calories a serving.

Yield: 4 servings

> 1 cup plain skim-milk yogurt
> 3 tablespoons lemon juice
> ⅓ cup dry white wine
> Grated rind of half a lemon
> 1 teaspoon vanilla
> Liquid artificial sweetener to taste
> 1 envelope unflavored gelatin
> ⅓ cup cold water
> 3 egg whites

Blend together the yogurt, lemon juice, wine, lemon rind, and vanilla. Add sweetener to taste.

Soak gelatin in cold water, place over low heat, and dissolve, stirring constantly. Fold into yogurt mixture; cool until thickened but not set.

Beat egg whites until stiff peaks form. Fold into thickened yogurt mixture. Divide into 4 dessert dishes; refrigerate until set. Just before serving, garnish each with a few cereal flakes and a sprig of mint.

raspberry dessert

A good recipe for using leftover egg yolks.

Yield: 4 servings

> 1 pint fresh raspberries
> ¼ cup sugar
> 2 to 3 tablespoons curaçao liquor
> 6 egg yolks
> 3 tablespoons confectioner's sugar
> ⅓ cup white wine
> 2 tablespoons raspberry liquor or rum
> 1 tablespoon lemon juice
> ½ cup plain yogurt

Wash and drain berries. Sprinkle with sugar; let stand 30 minutes. Divide between 4 glass sherbet or parfait dishes. Sprinkle with curaçao.

In top of a double boiler combine yolks, sugar, wine, liquor or rum, and lemon juice. Stir over simmering water only until thickened. Do not overheat. Stir in yogurt; pour over berries. Serve at once.

peach gelatin parfait

Elegant, but very easy to make.

Yield: 4 servings

> 1 3-ounce package peach* gelatin dessert mix
> 1 cup boiling water
> ½ cup plain yogurt
> ½ cup cold water
> Fresh or canned peach slices

Dissolve gelatin in boiling water. Remove ½ cup of this mixture and stir into yogurt. Pour into 4 parfait glasses; chill until firm, about 2 or 3 hours.

Add ½ cup cold water to remaining warm gelatin mixture. Let stand at room temperature.

When gelatin–yogurt mixture is firm, pour room-temperature mixture over it in the glasses. Chill until firm. Garnish with sliced peaches.

*Any other fruit flavor may be substituted.

Picture on opposite page: raspberry dessert

cantaloupe parfait

A delicious low-calorie summer dessert.

Yield: 4 servings

½ very ripe cantaloupe
Sugar or honey (optional)
2 to 3 cups plain yogurt

Chopped walnuts or sliced almonds
Sprigs of fresh mint leaves

Remove seeds and puree the pulp from the cantaloupe in a blender or food processor. Sweeten with sugar or honey to taste, if desired.

Alternate spoonfuls of yogurt and pureed cantaloupe in tall, clear parfait glasses. Top each with chopped nuts and a fresh sprig of mint, if available.

Note: Any other fresh fruit in season may be substituted for cantaloupe.

fruit and rice parfait

Yield: 6 to 8 servings

1 to 2 cups cold cooked rice
2 cups fruit-flavored yogurt
2 cups sliced fresh fruit, sweetened to taste with sugar or honey

Combine rice and yogurt. Spoon alternately with prepared fruit into parfait glasses. Garnish with whipped cream and a whole berry or with an orange or lemon twist or with a sprig of fresh mint leaves.

strawberries san remo

Yield: 4 servings

1 pint fresh strawberries, hulled, cleaned, and halved
3 tablespoons sugar

yogurt topping

3 egg yolks
⅓ cup sugar
1 teaspoon vanilla

Dash nutmeg
1 tablespoon brandy
2 cups plain yogurt

2 tablespoons sliced almonds
Shaved chocolate or chocolate sprinkles

Combine strawberries and sugar. Cover and let stand 15 minutes.

Prepare topping. Beat together yolks, sugar, vanilla, nutmeg, and brandy until smooth. Fold yogurt into this mixture.

Spoon strawberries into 4 sherbet dishes. Cover with topping and garnish with almonds and chocolate.

Picture on opposite page: strawberries san remo

strawberry ring mold

strawberry ring mold

Yield: 6 to 8 servings

    2 3-ounce packages strawberry gelatin dessert mix
    2 cups boiling water
    2 cups plain yogurt
    Grated rind of 1 lemon
    1 cup heavy cream, sweetened and whipped (garnish)
    Whole fresh strawberries (garnish)

Dissolve gelatin in boiling water. Cool; stir in yogurt and lemon rind. Pour into an 8-cup ring mold. Chill until firm.

Unmold onto a large serving dish. Garnish with whipped cream and fresh strawberries. Serve at once.

quickie pudding

Yield: 4 servings

> 1 3¾-ounce package your favorite instant pudding mix
> 1 cup milk
> 1 cup plain yogurt

Combine all ingredients; beat only until smooth. Pour at once into individual dessert dishes; refrigerate for 10 minutes before serving. Garnish with fresh fruit or nuts, if you wish.

vanilla tapioca pudding

Yield: 4 or 5 servings

> 3 tablespoons minute tapioca
> ⅓ cup sugar
> 1 beaten egg
> Dash salt
> 2 cups milk
> ¾ cup plain yogurt
> 1 teaspoon vanilla

Combine tapioca, sugar, egg, salt, and milk in a saucepan. Let stand 5 minutes to soften tapioca. Bring to a boil over moderately high heat, stirring constantly. Remove from heat; let cool slightly, about 10 minutes. Stir in yogurt and vanilla.

Spoon into dessert dishes. Serve warm or chilled, plain or topped with fruit and cinnamon or nutmeg.

chocolate pudding

Yield: 4 servings

> 1 package chocolate instant pudding
> 2 cups milk
> 1 cup plain yogurt
> 4 or 5 canned pear halves, drained and sliced
> 1 teaspoon grated lemon rind
> Chopped walnuts

Prepare pudding with milk according to package directions. Chill about 15 minutes, until set. Fold in yogurt, sliced pears, and lemon rind. Serve at once garnished with chopped walnuts.

sundae bar

Begin with a selection of:

Plain yogurt (lowest in calories)
Commercial fruit-flavored yogurt
Frozen Vanilla Yogurt I or II (see Index)

Set out an assortment of several of the following in small dishes to use as toppings:

**Sliced bananas, sprinkled with sugar and a little lemon juice to prevent
    browning**
Toasted shredded coconut
Assorted chopped dried fruits
Granola
Chopped nuts
Crushed peanut brittle
Raisins and nuts tossed with cinnamon and sugar
Toasted sesame seeds
Sliced fresh strawberries or frozen, defrosted strawberries
Wheat germ

eskimo apples

Yield: 6 servings

6 large red apples
Lemon juice
½ 10-ounce package frozen raspberries, thawed
2 tablespoons sugar
¼ cup raspberry liquor, rum, or kirsch
3 tablespoons flaked coconut
¼ cup ground almonds
½ cup plain yogurt
1 cup whipped cream or whipped topping (garnish)
Sliced almonds (garnish)

Wash apples well and polish with a clean towel. Cut off the top of each apple; brush with lemon juice to prevent discoloration. Set aside.

Carefully cut out the inside of each apple to leave a ½-inch shell. Brush the insides with lemon juice.

Dice the removed portions of the apples; discard the core and seeds. Combine with sugar, raspberries (reserve a few whole ones to use as a garnish), liquor, coconut, and ground almonds. Fold yogurt into this mixture. Spoon into apples.

Top each apple with a dollop of whipped cream, a reserved raspberry, and sliced almonds. Cover with apple tops and serve at once.

Picture on opposite page: eskimo apples

dessert crepes

Yield: 20 to 24

1 cup sifted all-purpose flour
3 eggs
1½ cups milk
1 tablespoon melted butter or margarine
¹/₈ teaspoon salt
2 tablespoons sugar
1 tablespoon brandy (optional)

Combine all ingredients; stir until completely blended. Allow batter to stand for 1 hour. The flour will absorb some of the liquid and the batter will be much easier to handle. Batter also may be refrigerated overnight.

Place 1 to 1½ tablespoons of the batter in the center of an electric frypan preheated to 380°F. Spread the batter quickly with the back of the spoon into a 6-inch circle.

Heat until lightly browned, about 1 minute. Turn with a spatula; heat about 1 minute longer.

Stack crepes as they are done. Fill with a selected filling at once or wrap tightly and store in the refrigerator for 1 to 2 days before filling. Crepes also may be frozen up to 2 months. Place a sheet of waxed paper between each.

When filling, remember to keep the side baked first facing the outside. This side is the most attractive.

fruit-filled crepes

Yield: About 20, to serve 4

1 cup plain yogurt
1 to 2 tablespoons sugar
4 large apples,* peeled, cored, and very thinly sliced
1 to 2 tablespoons lemon juice
20 Dessert Crepes
Cinnamon
Chopped nuts
Confectioner's sugar

Sweeten the yogurt with sugar.

Sprinkle apple slices with lemon juice and arrange in a row across the center of each crepe. Top each with about a tablespoon of yogurt. Roll up tightly.

Place on dessert plates and garnish with a dash of cinnamon, chopped nuts, and a sprinkling of confectioner's sugar.

*Other fresh fruits in season may be substituted for apples.

pastry for a single-crust pie

Yield: 1 9-inch pie shell

1¼ cups sifted all-purpose flour
½ teaspoon salt
½ cup hydrogenated shortening
3 to 4 tablespoons cold water or yogurt

Stir together the flour and salt. Cut in shortening until the pieces are the size of very coarse cornmeal. Sprinkle water or yogurt over this mixture and stir lightly with a fork until dough can be formed into a ball. Let rest about 10 minutes.

Roll out on a piece of floured waxed paper until crust is 1½ inches larger than the inverted pie pan. Ease dough into pan without stretching. Trim crust ½ inch beyond the edge of the pan and fold under to make a double thickness of dough around rim. Flute edge.

baked pie shell

Prick bottom and sides with a fork. Bake at 450°F on top shelf of oven for about 10 minutes.

pie shell to be filled before baking

Do not prick bottoms and sides. Fill and bake as recipe directs.

pastry for a double-crust pie

Yield: Pastry for a 9-inch double pie crust

2 cups sifted all-purpose flour
1 teaspoon salt
¾ cup hydrogenated shortening
¼ cup cold water or yogurt

Stir together the flour and salt. Cut in shortening until the pieces are the size of coarse cornmeal. Sprinkle water or yogurt over this mixture; stir with a fork until dough can be formed into a ball. Let rest about 10 minutes.

Divide dough in half; roll each half out separately until 1½ inches larger than the inverted pie pan. Line pan with one crust; trim edge even with pan rim. Fill pie. Top with second crust and fold edge under lower crust's rim. Crimp edge; bake according to recipe directions.

raisin pie

Try this with cut-up pitted prunes or dates in place of raisins.

Yield: 1 9-inch pie

¾ to 1 cup sugar
2 tablespoons cornstarch
½ teaspoon cinnamon
¼ teaspoon nutmeg
¼ teaspoon salt
1½ cups yogurt
3 egg yolks
1½ cups raisins

1½ tablespoons lemon juice
1 9-inch baked pie shell (see Index)

meringue topping

3 egg whites
¼ teaspoon cream of tartar
⅓ cup sugar
½ teaspoon vanilla

In a saucepan combine sugar, cornstarch, spices, salt, yogurt, yolks, raisins, and lemon juice. Place over moderately high heat; stir constantly until mixture comes to a full boil and has thickened. Pour into baked 9-inch pie shell.

Prepare Meringue Topping. Beat egg whites until frothy. Add cream of tartar. Continue to beat while adding sugar gradually. Beat until soft peaks form. Beat in vanilla.

Spread meringue over filling. Seal well to the edge of crust. Bake at 400°F for 4 to 5 minutes or until meringue is lightly browned. Cool at room temperature.

french apple pie

Yield: 1 9-inch pie

1 recipe Pastry for Double Crust Pie (see Index)
2 pounds cooking apples (about 6 medium), sliced
1 tablespoon lemon juice
2 tablespoons sugar
¼ teaspoon cinnamon
3 tablespoons butter or margarine

cream pie filling

2 tablespoons all-purpose flour
⅓ cup sugar
1 cup yogurt
3 egg yolks, lightly beaten
1 teaspoon vanilla
⅔ cup peach, raspberry, or apricot preserves

Prepare pastry according to recipe directions. Roll out half and line a 9-inch pie pan.

Combine apples, lemon juice, sugar, and cinnamon. Heat butter in a skillet. Add apples; sauté over moderate heat until nearly tender, about 4 minutes. Set aside.

Prepare cream filling. In a small saucepan stir together flour and sugar. Stir in yogurt. Heat over moderate heat, stirring constantly, until mixture boils and is thickened. Stir some of this hot mixture into the egg yolks. Stir this yolk mixture back into yogurt mixture. Stir in vanilla.

Pour cream filling into pie shell. Top with apple mixture. Dot with preserves.

Roll out second half of pastry into a 12-inch circle. Cut into ½-inch-wide strips. Arrange in a lattice pattern over filling. Tuck ends under rim of lower crust.

Bake at 400°F for 35 to 40 minutes. Do not over-bake, or cream filling may separate. Serve warm.

rainbow fruit pie

A beautiful, colorful dessert.

Yield: 1 9- or 10-inch tart

1 9- or 10-inch baked pie shell (see Index)

cream pie filling

⅓ **cup sugar**
1½ **tablespoons cornstarch**
Dash salt
1½ **cups plain yogurt**
3 egg yolks, lightly beaten
1 teaspoon vanilla extract
½ **teaspoon almond extract**

glaze

4 teaspoons cornstarch mixed with
 2 tablespoons cold water
1 cup water
2 tablespoons sugar
1 teaspoon lemon juice
Red food coloring

fruit topping

Fresh strawberries
Mandarin-orange sections
Seeded black grapes
Seeded green grapes

Prepare cream filling. In a small saucepan stir together the sugar, cornstarch, and salt. Blend in yogurt. Heat over moderate heat, stirring constantly, until mixture boils and is thickened. Stir a little of this hot mixture into the egg yolks. Stir egg-yolk mixture back into the yogurt mixture. Continue to cook, stirring constantly, until mixture thickens. Stir in vanilla and almond extracts. Refrigerate, covered with waxed paper to prevent formation of a skin, until chilled.

Pour cold filling into a cooled, baked pastry shell. Arrange fruit in an attractive pattern on top.

Prepare glaze. Combine glaze ingredients in a saucepan. Heat and stir until mixture boils and is clear. Tint a pale pink. Cool.

Pour cooled glaze over fruit-topped pie to cover completely. Refrigerate at least 1 hour before serving.

yummy cocoa frosting

For your favorite 2-layer white, yellow, or devil's food cake.

Yield: Frosting for a 2-layer 8-inch cake

¼ **pound butter**
1 pound confectioner's sugar
⅔ **cup cocoa**

¼ **teaspoon salt**
1½ **teaspoons vanilla**
⅓ **cup yogurt (approximately)**

Cream butter until light and fluffy. Stir in remaining ingredients; beat until smooth.

Frost sides and top of cake when cake is completely cool. If you wish, garnish with slivered almonds or pistachio nuts.

lemon–rum cake with wine syrup

Yield: 1 10-inch cake

¾ cup butter
1½ cups sugar
6 egg yolks
1 teaspoon grated lemon rind
1 teaspoon vanilla
1¾ cups yogurt
¼ cup rum
2 cups sifted cake flour
4 teaspoons baking powder
½ teaspoon salt
½ teaspoon almond extract
6 egg whites
½ cup chopped almonds

wine syrup

1 cup dry red wine
½ cup sugar
½ teaspoon cinnamon
Dash cloves

Cream together the butter, sugar, egg yolks, rind, and vanilla until light and fluffy.

Combine yogurt and rum.

Sift together flour, baking powder, and salt.

Add dry ingredients to creamed mixture alternately with yogurt–rum mixture. Stir after each addition. Beat for 1 minute, until mixture is light.

Combine almond extract with egg whites; beat until stiff, but not dry. Fold gently into the cake batter along with the almonds.

Pour into a 10-inch tube pan; bake at 350°F for about 30 minutes. Cool for 10 minutes. Remove from pan; cool on wire rack.

Combine ingredients for Wine Syrup; simmer over low heat for about 5 minutes. Cool; pour in a thin stream over the cake. Let stand about an hour before serving.

nut puffs

Yield: About 2 or 3 dozen

2 cups sifted all-purpose flour
¼ cup sugar
1 teaspoon baking powder
½ teaspoon baking soda
1 teaspoon salt
1 teaspoon nutmeg
¼ cup vegetable oil
1 egg
¾ cup plain yogurt
1 cup confectioner's sugar
⅓ cup boiling water
Finely chopped nuts

Sift together the flour, sugar, baking powder, baking soda, salt, and nutmeg.

Stir together the vegetable oil, egg, and yogurt. Add these liquid ingredients to the dry ingredients; mix with a fork until well-blended.

Drop batter by heaping teaspoonfuls into hot (375°F) oil. Deep-fry about 3 minutes or until golden. Drain on paper towels.

Combine confectioner's sugar and water to make a glaze. Dip warm puffs in glaze and roll in chopped nuts. Serve while still warm.

Puffs may be rolled in granulated sugar rather than in the glaze.

cheesecake

Yield: 1 8- or 9-inch cheesecake

crust

8 ounces graham cracker or zwieback crumbs
2 tablespoons sugar
Pinch salt
¼ cup butter

cheesecake filling

⅓ cup butter
¼ cup sugar
4 egg yolks
1 teaspoon vanilla
¼ teaspoon salt

⅓ cup flour
12 ounces cream cheese
½ cup plain yogurt
4 egg whites

Prepare crust. Combine crumbs, sugar, salt, and butter. Knead into a dough. Press mixture evenly over the bottom and up the sides of an 8- or 9-inch springform pan or pie pan.

Prepare filling. Beat butter and sugar together until light. Beat in yolks, vanilla, and salt. Sprinkle flour over mixture and stir it in. Add cream cheese and yogurt. Stir until well-blended.

Beat egg whites until stiff peaks form; fold into the cream-cheese mixture. Pour into prepared crumb crust. Bake at 350°F for 50 to 60 minutes. Cool in pan before serving.

susan's oatmeal cookies

Yield: 5 or 6 dozen

¾ cup hydrogenated shortening
1 cup sugar
2 eggs
2 tablespoons molasses
1½ cups sifted all-purpose flour
1 teaspoon cinnamon
¼ teaspoon nutmeg

1 teaspoon baking powder
½ teaspoon salt
¼ cup plain yogurt
3 cups rolled oats
½ cup raisins
½ cup coarsely chopped walnuts

Combine shortening, sugar, and eggs. Beat until very light and fluffy. Beat in the molasses.

Sift together flour, spices, baking powder, and salt. Add to the creamed mixture along with the yogurt. Stir until combined. Stir in oats, raisins, and walnuts.

Drop heaping teaspoons of the batter 2 inches apart on ungreased baking sheets. Bake on the top oven shelf at 350°F for 12 to 15 minutes or until a light, golden brown. Cool on wire racks.

Picture on next page: cheesecake

quick breads

cornbread

Yield: 6 servings

1 cup all-purpose flour
1 cup cornmeal
¼ cup sugar
½ teaspoon baking soda
½ teaspoon salt
1 cup plain yogurt
¼ cup vegetable oil
1 egg

Stir together the flour, cornmeal, sugar, soda, and salt.
Combine yogurt, oil, and egg. Beat until smooth.
Stir yogurt mixture into dry ingredients. Stir only until dry ingredients are moistened.
Pour into an 8-inch-square baking pan. Bake at 400°F for about 20 minutes. Serve while still warm.

health muffins

Yield: 12 muffins

¾ cup sifted all-purpose flour
¼ teaspoon salt
3 teaspoons baking powder
¼ cup raisins
½ cup peanut butter
¼ cup butter or margarine
¼ cup brown sugar
1 egg
1 cup bran breakfast cereal
½ cup plain yogurt
¼ cup milk

Sift together the flour, salt, and baking powder. Stir in raisins.
Cream together the peanut butter, butter, brown sugar, and egg. Stir in bran, yogurt, and milk until well-blended. Add the dry ingredients and stir only until moistened.
Drop batter into lightly greased muffin tins. Fill each about ⅔ full. Bake at 400°F for about 20 minutes.

whole-wheat muffins

Yield: 12 muffins

1 cup whole-wheat flour
1 cup sifted all-purpose flour
1 teaspoon salt
3 teaspoons baking powder
½ teaspoon baking soda
3 tablespoons sugar
3 tablespoons vegetable oil
1 egg
1 cup plain yogurt

Sift together the flours, salt, baking powder, baking soda, and sugar.

Stir together the oil, egg, and yogurt. Add these liquid ingredients to the dry ingredients all at once. Stir only enough to barely moisten the dry ingredients. Batter should be lumpy.

Fill greased muffin cups two-thirds full. Bake at 400°F for 15 to 20 minutes.

muffin variations

Add ½ to 1 cup of any one of the following just before stirring in liquid ingredients:

Diced apple
Shredded apricots
Blueberries
Shredded cheese
Chopped dates
Nuts—walnuts or pecans
Raisins

beverages

apricot delight

Yield: About 2 cups

½ cup plain yogurt
½ cup apricot nectar
1 banana, cut up

3 or 4 ice cubes
Dash nutmeg

Combine all ingredients in blender; blend until smooth. Serve at once.

orange delight

orange delight

Yield: About 1½ cups

½ cup orange juice
1 tablespoon lemon juice
2 tablespoons honey
1 cup plain yogurt
Orange peel (garnish)

Combine and shake all ingredients except peel.
Pour into a tall glass. Garnish rim with a curled strip of orange peel (or slice of orange).

summer pear cooler

Yield: About 2 cups

2 canned pear halves, chilled
¼ cup pear juice from canned pears
1 cup plain yogurt

¼ cup rum
Scant teaspoon strawberry or
raspberry preserves

In a blender puree pears and pear juice. Add yogurt and rum. Blend until smooth. Pour into a tall glass. Top with preserves.

137

banana shake

Yield: 3 cups

 1 banana
 1 tablespoon lemon juice
 4 tablespoons sugar
 1 cup milk
 1 cup plain yogurt
 Whipped cream (garnish)

banana shake

Puree banana, lemon juice, and sugar in a blender until smooth. Add milk and yogurt; continue blending until thoroughly mixed.

Pour at once into glasses. Top with a dab of whipped cream.

berry shake

Yield: 4 servings

 1 10-ounce package frozen strawberries or raspberries
 2 or 3 cups plain yogurt

Cut or break block of frozen fruit into 1-inch chunks. Place in blender jar with yogurt. Blend until smooth and frothy.

Serve shake at once or pack in insulated individual containers for lunch.

orange ice-cream shake

Yield: 4 servings

 3 cups plain yogurt
 1 cup frozen vanilla yogurt or vanilla ice cream
 ⅓ cup orange-flavored breakfast-drink mix

Combine all ingredients in a blender jar; blend until smooth. Garnish with a sprig of mint or a dash of cinnamon or nutmeg.

strawberry or blueberry shake

Yield: About 2 cups

 1 cup plain yogurt
 ½ to ¾ cup fresh strawberries or blueberries
 1 to 2 tablespoons honey
 4 ice cubes

Combine all ingredients in a blender; blend until smooth. Enjoy at once.

strawberry shake

vanilla shake with chartreuse

vanilla shake with chartreuse

Yield: About 1½ cups

1 cup plain yogurt
2 scoops vanilla ice cream

2 tablespoons chartreuse (a French liquor)
Maraschino cherry (garnish)

Blend first 3 ingredients until smooth in a blender.
Pour into a glass and garnish with a cherry on a toothpick.

chocolate malt

Yield: About 3 cups

2 cups plain yogurt
¼ cup chocolate syrup

2 tablespoons malted-milk powder
1 cup vanilla ice cream

Place all ingredients in a blender jar; blend until smooth and frothy.
Pour into tall glasses and serve at once.

strawberry shake

Yield: About 2 cups

½ cup (or more) strawberries
2 tablespoons honey
1 cup cold milk

1 cup plain yogurt
Large whole strawberries (garnish)

Puree ½ cup strawberries and honey in a blender. Add milk and yogurt; blend until smooth.
Pour into glasses and garnish each with a whole strawberry.

holiday eggnog

Yield: 1 gallon, to serve 16 to 40

12 egg whites	4 cups plain yogurt
2 cups sugar	1 fifth cold bourbon
12 egg yolks	½ cup cold rum
1 quart light cream	Dash nutmeg

Beat egg whites until foamy. Gradually add 1 cup of the sugar while beating until soft peaks form. Set aside.

Beat egg yolks until light. Gradually beat in remaining cup of sugar.

Fold beaten whites into beaten yolks. Add cream, yogurt, bourbon, and rum. Stir gently.

Pour into punch bowl and dust with nutmeg.

creme de menthe pickup

Yield: About 1 cup, to serve 2 persons

1 tablespoon grenadine	½ cup plain yogurt
Sugar	¼ cup creme de menthe
½ cup cold milk	2 tablespoons cointreau

Pour grenadine in a small, shallow bowl.

Place sugar in a second dish.

Dip rims of glasses in grenadine, then in sugar.

In a blender, blend milk, yogurt, creme de menthe, and cointreau until smooth.

Pour into prepared glasses and serve immediately.

chocolate brandy

Yield: About 1½ cups

2 scoops chocolate ice cream	Whipped cream (garnish)
1 cup plain yogurt	Cocoa (garnish)
2 tablespoons brandy	

Place ice cream, yogurt, and brandy in blender; blend until smooth. Pour into a tall glass. Garnish with whipped cream and a pinch of cocoa.

creme de menthe pickup

chocolate brandy

grape frost

Frothy and refreshing.

Yield: About 2½ cups

1 cup grape juice
1 cup plain yogurt
4 or 5 ice cubes

Place all ingredients in blender; blend until smooth. Serve at once.

lemon–lime cooler

Yield: 3 cups

2 cups plain yogurt
2 tablespoons lemon juice
2 tablespoons lime juice

2 tablespoons honey or sugar
4 ice cubes

Place all ingredients in a blender jar; blend until smooth. Serve immediately.

piña colada

Yield: About 2 cups

1 cup plain yogurt
½ cup coconut juice (available canned)
½ cup pineapple juice

2 to 3 tablespoons honey or sugar
4 or 5 ice cubes
¼ cup rum (optional)

Combine all ingredients in a blender jar; blend until smooth. Serve at once.

index